GRIEF, FORGIVENESS, ACCEPTANCE, AND REJECTION

GRIEF, FORGIVENESS, ACCEPTANCE, AND REJECTION

DR. DANIEL BRUBAKER

Copyright © 2024 Dr. Daniel Brubaker.

All rights reserved. No part of this book may be used or reproduced by any means, graphic, electronic, or mechanical, including photocopying, recording, taping or by any information storage retrieval system without the written permission of the author except in the case of brief quotations embodied in critical articles and reviews.

This book is a work of non-fiction. Unless otherwise noted, the author and the publisher make no explicit guarantees as to the accuracy of the information contained in this book and in some cases, names of people and places have been altered to protect their privacy.

Archway Publishing books may be ordered through booksellers or by contacting:

Archway Publishing
1663 Liberty Drive
Bloomington, IN 47403
www.archwaypublishing.com
844-669-3957

Because of the dynamic nature of the Internet, any web addresses or links contained in this book may have changed since publication and may no longer be valid. The views expressed in this work are solely those of the author and do not necessarily reflect the views of the publisher, and the publisher hereby disclaims any responsibility for them.

Any people depicted in stock imagery provided by Getty Images are models, and such images are being used for illustrative purposes only. Certain stock imagery © Getty Images.

Holy Bible, New International Version®, NIV® Copyright ©1973, 1978, 1984, 2011 by Biblica, Inc.® Used by permission. All rights reserved worldwide.

The Holy Bible, English Standard Version. ESV® Text Edition: 2016. Copyright © 2001 by Crossway Bibles, a publishing ministry of Good News Publishers.

ISBN: 978-1-6657-6315-8 (sc)
ISBN: 978-1-6657-6316-5 (hc)
ISBN: 978-1-6657-6317-2 (e)

Library of Congress Control Number: 2024914847

Print information available on the last page.

Archway Publishing rev. date: 07/30/2024

DEDICATIONS

To all murder victims, and their families, friends, and loved ones.
To all military wounded warriors and loved ones
To all victims of hate speech and hate crimes.
To my son, a first responder, firefighter, and
emergency medical technician.
To my wife, who has grieved over the
death of her mother and father.
To my associate, assistant nurse, and
friend for what she does for me

CONTENTS

About the Author ix
Introduction xi

Chapter 1   Crying 1
Chapter 2   Grief 30
Chapter 3   Forgiveness 55
Chapter 4   Grief Acceptance, Personal Acceptance and
            Perseverance 97
Chapter 5   Social Acceptance and Rejection by
            Other People 116
Chapter 6   Social Acceptance and Rejection of
            Other People 135
Chapter 7   Extreme Rejection; Hate 155
Chapter 8   Conclusion of Grief and Forgiveness 185

ABOUT THE AUTHOR

Daniel B. Brubaker, DO, obtained his Doctorate of Osteopathy (DO) from the Philadelphia College of Osteopathic Medicine in 1974. His postgraduate training (residency) was at the University of Pittsburgh Health Center in pathology. He completed three American Board of Pathology certifications. He spent thirty years in academic medicine at Oklahoma University Health Science Center, University of California, Los Angeles Medical Center, and University of California, San Francisco. He has written in several medical journals, chapters in textbooks, and nonfiction books.

A doctor of osteopathic medicine is a fully trained and licensed doctor. A Doctor of Osteopathic Medicine graduates from an American osteopathic medical school. A Doctor of Medicine (MD) graduates from a traditional medical school. DOs have the same traditional courses in medicine as MDs and additional training in neuromuscular medicine. Osteopathic manual therapy focuses on relieving pain and tension in the musculoskeletal system. DOs are fully licensed physicians who practice in all areas and specialties of medicine, and they are philosophically trained to use a whole-person approach to partner with their patients.

What does Dr. Brubaker know about grieving? Dr. Brubaker transitioned from academic medicine to private practice in 2000. Most of his practice involves patients with injuries and—to a lesser extent—general medicine, which includes patients with cancer. Injured and cancer patients undergo a grieving process, and their families do too. Dr. Brubaker has also dealt with personal and health problems. He survived stage 4 colon cancer more than twenty-two years ago, and he has had two episodes of melanoma, eight spine surgeries, and more than twenty-four surgeries and laser treatments on his eyes for glaucoma.

For Dr. Brubaker, the most difficult part of the grieving process has been the slow progression of vision loss due to advanced glaucoma.

INTRODUCTION

This book centers on grief, forgiveness, acceptance, and rejection, but chapter 1 starts with crying. Crying is mostly associated with grief, but it can be associated with happiness too. It also occurs with several other emotions, such as anger, fear, anxiety, and depression. To understand crying in different emotions, it is helpful to understand the biology of crying.

Humans are the only animal that cries. It is a function of the brain that allows us to release horrific emotions. American troops who marched through the concentration camps of World War II could not hide their crying after what they saw. Hatred, torture, and death—and less severe conditions like divorce or getting fired from a job—can all lead to crying. Although crying is only a function of humans, grief is not.

In chapter 2, grief is discussed in detail. Grief is the constellation or spectrum of internal thoughts and feelings when there is primary grief (such as the loss of a job or a divorce) or secondary grief (when someone we love dies). Grief is the internal meaning given to the experience of loss. Mourning is outwardly expressing internal grief. Grief occurs in stages, but it does not necessarily occur in a specific order. Being aware of the grief process can help people cope with their grief. Awareness of the severity of grief can be very useful.

Grief occurs in all mammals. When a mother caribou watches her calf being killed by wolves, we can see her grief. The other animals in the herd come to her aid.

The process of forgiveness is similar to the grieving process because of the psychosocial behaviors and length of time to process the emotions. Chapter 3 is an attempt to evaluate and understand forgiveness. Forgiveness is as old as ancient times, and it can be found in the oldest religion, Hinduism. Forgiveness can be found in all religions. Forgiveness is a complex psychosocial emotion, and many areas in the brain are involved in forgiveness. Forgiveness is an emotion-focused coping strategy that can reduce stress. The goal of forgiveness is to eliminate anger, hostility, and resentment. Chapter 3 provides ways to do this and mechanisms to adjust to situations where forgiveness may not come to fruition. The purpose of this chapter is to create awareness of the psychosocial aspects of forgiveness.

Chapter 4 addresses personal acceptance and rejection. Acceptance in the grieving process is the last stage of Elizabeth Kübler-Ross's five stages of grief: *denial, anger, bargaining, depression, and acceptance* (DABDA). We have added *shock* as the first stage and *moving on* as the last stage. The seven stages of grief—shock, denial, anger, bargaining, depression, acceptance, and moving on—do not need to occur in a particular order. A person may only go through a few stages. For example, when I was diagnosed with stage 4 colon cancer in 2000, I went from denial to moving on and skipped all the other stages.

Chapter 4 also evaluates methods for accomplishing acceptance. Grief may include anxiety and depression. Mindfulness training can help a person overcome some of the negative aspects of grief and help achieve acceptance. Counseling and therapy can also help a person overcome grief, which can lead to acceptance and moving on.

Social acceptance is defined as the outcome of a collective judgment or a collective project, plan, or policy. A collective judgment can be positive or negative, and it is never set in time. Social acceptance means that other people wish to include another person in their group or relationship. Social acceptance occurs on a continuum that ranges from merely tolerating a person's behavior to disliking that person.

Social acceptance is more complex than self-acceptance. It includes acceptance by peers and other groups. It can include political, religious, gender, sexual, environmental, technological or other types of acceptance. In this context, one can easily appreciate the complexity of social acceptance. Social acceptance has dual meanings, and I have divided social acceptance into accepted by others (chapter 5) and accepting others (chapter 6).

In chapter 5, social acceptance by others is defined as the degree to which an individual is actively brought into social interactions by others (in individual and/or group relationships).

Acceptance by parents is the first stage in self-acceptance. Positive acceptance by parents leads to self-esteem in a child. This usually leads to acceptance by peers. Everyone wants some form of acceptance; as human beings, that is part of our existence. Rejection in early stages can lead to mental health issues, and when mental health issues arise, meditation, prayer, and other techniques can be helpful. The psychosocial issues involved with adult rejection can be problematic and include ostracism and cancel culture.

Chapter 6 addresses psychosocial behaviors in accepting and/or rejecting other people. This applies to a person's inner circle and their outer circle. A person's inner circle is made up of family, friends, and loved ones, which has a different psychological impact, such as personality traits. The outer circle is more complex psychologically, philosophically, and socially. This form of acceptance involves ethics and morality. Chapter 6 includes a detailed analysis of the morality of accepting others. Anyone wanting to work on accepting others should learn about the morality of acceptance, including tolerance and respect.

The counterpart to social acceptance- is social rejection. Rejection can cause grieving, and the intention of this book is to go full circle in the process of grieving. Social rejection can mean anything from detachment from a mother as a baby to hatred as an adult. Although one does not think of separation of an unwanted baby or child as causing grief in the child, the child experiences loss without cognition. The child's emotions are the same as in grieving.

Chapter 7 discusses the rejection of others in the form of hate. Hate can indirectly cause grief. The grieving process applies to the victims and their loved ones.

Let us consider bullying in schools, and politics. As an example, a strong, aggressive child in school, bully's another innocent or weaker child. The bully finds pleasure in overpowering his victim causing either physical or verbal pain. This causes a grieving process in the victim in the form of crying, denial, depression, and eventually anger. Eventually, the anger over time turns into hate in the victim child who may seek revenge and retaliate when he becomes older and stronger. Here, it is most likely that hate is evident in both the one who inflicts pain and the one who suffers.

Alex Jones, a far-right political media mogul, spreads conspiracy theories and told his audience that the Sandy Hook Elementary School shooting never happened. He claimed it was all a hoax manufactured by the children's parents. As a result, the parents were threatened by members of his audience. These parents were still grieving ten years after the shooting, and causing more mental harm was extremely cruel. Lawsuits by the families resulted in a cumulative judgment of a billion dollars for defamation.

Hatred has severe consequences for all parties. This emotion can be directed to individuals, groups, or objects that cause discomfort or pain. Hate is often associated with feelings of anger, disgust, or deep disappointment toward those who are hostile to us. Hate can cause grief, which can cause more hate. It rarely causes forgiveness.

Chapter 8 further discusses and summarizes grief and forgiveness. There is an overlap between the two grief and forgiveness, and they both require the same coping skills. A person may require professional help if grief interferes with their ability to function.

There is so much hate, pain, and suffering in our lives, but this book can help us all break through our negative emotions and find happiness.

CHAPTER 1
CRYING

Crying is a complex formation of tears. Physiologically, they come from the lacrimal gland in the eye in response to emotions: sadness, pain, loss, loneliness, anger, and even happiness. Sobbing is considered loud crying.

This chapter describes the biology behind crying. The purpose is to understand the mechanism of crying in each emotion.

TYPES OF TEARS

There are three types of tears: basal tears, emotional tears, and reflex tears. All are produced by the lacrimal glands around the eye, and all are needed for good eye health.

Basal production of tears has to do with the bottom layer of tears that wet the eyes, allowing one to blink and see clearly. Dry eyes cause pain and blurred vision. According to the American Academy of Ophthalmology (AAO), a person makes fifteen to thirty gallons of tears every year.

Emotional tears come as a result of various emotions, which are fabricated from chemicals in the brain.

Reflex tears occur as a result of an external stimulant to the lacrimal glands. Examples are tears when peeling onions or peppers. Medical issues such as an infection or ulcer of the cornea can also cause tearing.

Crying in this chapter only involves emotional tears.

THEORIES CONCERNING EMOTIONAL CRYING

There are a number of psychological theories concerning the etiology of crying. Earlier theories stated that crying is a precondition to cognitively becoming aware of emotions such as fear or anger, but it seems more reasonable to propose that crying is a response to fear or anger.

Recent psychological theories suggest that crying may be showing submissiveness, helplessness, or resolving feelings of grief. Evolutionary theorists believe the function of crying is to fill the eyes with tears so as to not be able to see, blurring the eyes to the oncoming attack. In this respect, crying creates vulnerability and submission to an attacker, solicits sympathy or aid from bystanders, and signals shared emotional attachments.

BIOLOGICAL BENEFITS OF CRYING

Emotional crying is biologically complex due to the involvement of hormones and neurochemicals. Crying releases several chemicals and hormones that can affect the parasympathetic nervous system, which is responsible for heart rate, breathing, and other functions that are automatic in the body. Crying stimulates the parasympathetic nervous system to decrease heart rate and breathing. It provides a soothing effect and calms emotions. As a result, with support from others, the crying person relaxes as an attachment behavior.

Crying may lift people's spirits and make them feel better. The calming, mood-enhancing, and pain-relieving effects of crying also may help a person fall asleep more easily. Oxytocin and endorphins can help improve mood. This is why they are often known as "feel-good chemicals."

Crying helps relieve pain. This encompasses the endocannabinoids, also called endogenous cannabinoids, which are molecules made by the body. They're similar to the cannabinoids in the cannabis plant. Experts have identified two key endocannabinoids so far: CBD and anandamide.

Endocannabinoids are signaling molecules that help regulate various processes, such as pain, memory, mood, immunity, and stress. CBD does, however, interact with other receptors, such as serotonin and opioid receptors.

The endocannabinoids system (ECS) is a complex nerve cell signaling system that modulates the central nervous system's function and helps maintain homeostasis.

Oxytocin is typically linked to warm, fuzzy feelings and is shown in some research to lower stress and anxiety. Oxytocin has the power to regulate our emotional responses and prosocial behaviors, including trust, empathy, gazing, positive memories, processing of bonding cues, and positive communication.

Endorphins are complex proteins (polypeptides) made by the pituitary gland and central nervous system. Endorphins primarily help one deal with stress and reduce feelings of psychological or physical pain. In terms of psychological pain, the pleasure effect associated with endorphins is in part related to the increased dopamine production that occurs due to endorphin activity. In terms of physical pain, endorphins also trigger a positive feeling in the body, similar to that of morphine. Therefore, endorphins are released in response to pain or stress, but they are also released during other activities, like eating, exercise, sex, and crying.

Prolactin is a hormone found in the pituitary, which is involved in milk production at birth. However, it has also been found to stimulate crying. It increases during stress, causing crying in women and men.

The parasympathetic system is also involved in crying. Acetylcholine, a neurochemical produced by the parasympathetic nervous system, stimulates the lacrimal glands—the glands around the eyes that secrete tears.

The sympathetic nervous system is involved with crying that is related to fear.

SOCIOLOGY OF CRYING

Gender, class, culture, age, religious rituals, symbolism, and occupational roles, for instance, can all affect the meaning of crying.

GENDER AND CRYING

A report in a German ophthalmology journal, "Women and Men Cry Differently," showed gender differences in crying (*Deutsche Ophtalmologische Gesellschaft*, October 2009). The average woman cries between thirty and sixty-four times a year, and the average man cries between six and seventeen times a year. However, in the author's experience, men tend to cry just as much as women or more. Men tend to cry for between two and four minutes, and women cry for about six minutes. Crying turns into sobbing for women in 65 percent of cases, compared to just 6 percent for men. Until adolescence, however, no difference between the sexes was found.

SYMBOLIC AND RITUALISTIC CRYING

Crying has forever played an important role as a symbol and ritual in religions around the world. Crying has been involved in diverse symbolic religious traditions, and it has many uses in religious rituals.

Muslims religiously cry for their love of Muhammad. Shia Muslims cry during the annual remembrance of the martyrdom of al-Husayn. For Christians, crying is thought to be sacramental and helpful in forgiving sins in that they recall the "baptism of the penitence."

In Buddhism, crying is a sign of being strong. Crying is a reaction to suffering, and the goal of Buddhist practice is to be free from suffering. You may cry during your practice, and it's normal for a worldling to cry, but a fully enlightened one will not cry because they are beyond suffering. For a supposedly dispassionate Buddhist monk, for instance, crying over a death might be considered inappropriate, but this would not bring any censure for a layperson. The weeping Buddha symbolizes Buddha crying for the suffering of the world and his angst for the persistent sorrow in our lives. Rubbing Buddha's back on a statue gives peace and strength. It is believed it will take away your pain and be a source of happiness and joy in your life.

The symbolism of crying is not limited to religion. Many cultures in the past and present have symbolic crying. As an example, the Aztecs had a ritual of crying. During the annual dry season, as well as in periods of extended drought, the Aztecs performed rain rituals, which incorporated sacrifice and ritual weeping. The ritual tears flowed down, causing the release and counterflow of fresh productive water from underworld springs.

Symbolic weeping occurs today in America. Music, movies, stories, and nature are other examples of where symbolic weeping can be found. Observing a famous singer singing the *Star-Spangled Banner* with an American flag in the background can cause tears to roll down cheeks. The crying could be due to joy about living in a free country, thinking of those who died to protect our freedom, or fearing that freedom could be lost.

TYPES OF CRYING—NEGATIVE AND POSITIVE

Negative and positive crying can be thought of on a spatial dimension. Negative crying is associated with distance, where the crying occurs with someone's death, and positive crying is a result of a close presence to someone or something. An example is when a mother cries at her child's graduation.

Another dimension is known as the public-private perspective. This describes two types of crying as ways to imply details about the self to the self or others. For example, crying due to a loss is a message to the outside world that pleads for help in coping with internal suffering. Sorrowful crying is a method of self-pity or self-regard; it is a way to comforts oneself. Joyful crying, in contrast, is recognition of beauty, glory, or wonderfulness.

Positive and negative crying are emotionally dependent. Different emotions cause crying, only if the emotion reaches a level that is severely experiential. A person may cry at a mother's death but not a father's death; it is dependent upon the relationship. Negative crying can be severe in a person who was extremely close to their mother, but in other situations, the reverse may be true. A person with sadness may not cry, but when the sadness becomes more emotional, the person will cry. Being at a joyful event like a child's graduation may cause a parent to shed tears, especially if the two have a close relationship. One could also describe this dimension as situational crying.

CATEGORIZATION OF CRYING

Crying should not be considered a psychological theory; it is an emotional physiological response. Different emotions can cause crying anywhere from fear to happiness. These emotions could be immediate or occur periodically.

Crying can be considered immediate (acute) or recurring (chronic) in response to emotions. Babies have chronic crying because they are unable to express their needs.

CATEGORIES OF EMOTIONAL CRYING

The symptoms commonly overlap in stress, anxiety, fear, or anger. The difference between these emotions depends on whether they are immediate or long-lasting events. Acute stress, anxiety, anger, and fear are immediate responses, whereas anxiety and some forms of stress are longer-lasting on the body.

FEAR, ANGER, STRESS, AND ANXIETY

Fear, anger, stress, and anxiety often occur together, but the terms are not interchangeable. The physiology and resulting symptoms commonly overlap. The difference is determined by a person's experiences. The emotions are based on the context of the events and circumstances. Fear relates to a known or understood threat, and anxiety follows from an unknown or poorly defined threat. Fear, anger, and stress are immediate (acute), and anxiety lasts longer (chronic). Stress can be considered an immediate or long-lasting condition (see definitions to distinguish all four). The differences can account for how people react to adverse or dangerous events.

Anxiety is an unpleasant feeling or vague sense of apprehension. It's often a response to an imprecise or unknown threat, such as the uneasiness you might feel walking down a dark street alone.

Anger, fear, anxiety, and stress can stimulate crying. All four of these emotions have similar biological mechanisms:

- Anger is a strong feeling of displeasure, annoyance, or hostility.
- Stress is a state of mental or emotional strain or tension, resulting from adverse or demanding circumstances.
- Fear is an unpleasant emotion caused by someone or something dangerous and is likely to cause pain or other harm.
- Anxiety is a feeling of worry, nervousness, or unease about an imminent event or an uncertain outcome.

BIOLOGICAL PHYSIOLOGY OF THE FIGHT-OR-FLIGHT RESPONSE (SYMPATHETIC STRESS RESPONSE)

The autonomic nervous system is a control system that acts largely unconsciously and regulates bodily functions, such as heart rate, digestion, respiratory rate, pupillary response, urination, and sexual arousal. This system is the primary mechanism in control of the fight-or-flight response.

The body's biological response to immediate stress, anxiety, anger, or fear is called the fight-or-flight response; it is also known as *acute sympathetic stress response*. When there is a perceived threat or danger to a person, the part of the brain that responds is the amygdala. Fearful and dangerous visual images and audible sounds trigger and activate the amygdala. This has been proven by several brain imaging research studies using positron emission tomography (PET) and functional magnetic resonance imaging (fMRI).

The amygdala is the central area of the brain for the fight-or-flight response. This response is triggered by emotions like fear, anxiety, aggression, and anger. In the amygdala, dopamine is involved with processes, especially those involving behavioral responses to rewarding or adverse stimuli. In adverse situations, such as danger, the amygdala sends messages to the hypothalamus, which initiates stimulation to the sympathetic nervous system.

The thalamus collects sensory data from the senses: eyes (sight, observation), ears (hearing), smell, and taste. The thalamus receives the information and processes it, sending the data to the sensory cortex where it is processed and interpreted. The cortex organizes information for dissemination to the hypothalamus (fight-or-flight), amygdala (fear), and hippocampus (memory).

The brain structures that are the center of most neurobiological events associated with fear are the two amygdalae, located behind the pituitary gland. Each amygdala is part of a circuitry of fear learning. They are essential for proper adaptation to stress and specific modulation of emotional learning memory. In the presence of a threatening stimulus, the amygdalae generate the secretion of hormones that influence fear and aggression. When the stimulus for fear or aggression commences, the amygdalae may elicit the release of hormones into the body to put the person into a state of alertness, in which they are ready to move, run, fight, and all types of sympathetic responses. This fight-or-flight response is regulated by the hypothalamus and the limbic system.

The sympathetic nervous system activates the fight-or-flight response. The sympathetic nervous system is made up of the hypothalamus, which has nerve pathways from the hypothalamus down the spinal cord to ganglia located near the spine and also pathways to the adrenal glands (called the hypothalamus-adrenal HA axis). The sympathetic nervous system is therefore made up of the hypothalamus, the spinal cord pathway, the sympathetic ganglia on both sides of the vertebrae, and the adrenal gland.

The sympathetic nervous system operates through a series of interconnected nerves (neurons). The sympathetic ganglia are close to nerves leaving the spinal cord. The connection from the spinal cord to the ganglia is called pre-ganglia, and the nerves that leave the ganglia are called the post-ganglia, now part of the peripheral nervous system.

The sympathetic nerves are also part of the peripheral nervous system (nerves from the spinal cord to organs and tissues like muscles). The ganglia are part of the peripheral nervous system.

When an electrical wire is connected to another, there is usually an on-and-off switch. The same is true for nerves. A nerve connects to another nerve, and the on-off switch is called a synapse. When the nerve stimulates another nerve, it is done through a chemical transmitter, which is called a neurotransmitter. At synapses within the sympathetic ganglia, preganglionic sympathetic nerves release the neurotransmitter, acetylcholine, a chemical messenger that binds and activates nicotinic acetylcholine receptors on postganglionic nerves (neurons). In response to this stimulus, postganglionic neurons principally release noradrenaline (norepinephrine). Prolonged activation can elicit the release of adrenaline (epinephrine) from the adrenal gland medulla. Norepinephrine and epinephrine are also called catecholamines.

Once released, norepinephrine and epinephrine bind to receptors, called adrenergic receptors, on peripheral tissues. Binding to adrenergic receptors causes the effects seen during the fight-or-flight response. These include pupil dilation, increased sweating, increased heart rate, increased blood pressure, and increased breathing.

The two main neurochemicals are epinephrine (also known as adrenaline) and norepinephrine. Cortisol is also a hormone that is produced. All three are produced in the adrenal glands, which are located above the kidneys. Epinephrine and norepinephrine are also produced in the brain stem. They can affect the breathing center in the midbrain.

SYMPATHETIC SYMPTOMS

- acceleration of heart and lung action
- increase in blood pressure
- paling or flushing, or alternating between both
- sweating
- inhibition of stomach and upper-intestinal action to the point where digestion slows down or stops

GENERAL EFFECT ON THE SPHINCTERS OF THE BODY

- constriction of blood vessels in many parts of the body
- liberation of nutrients (particularly fat and glucose) for muscular action
- dilation of blood vessels for muscles
- inhibition of the lacrimal gland (responsible for tear production) and salivation
- dilation of pupil (mydriasis)
- relaxation of bladder
- inhibition of erection
- auditory exclusion (loss of hearing)
- tunnel vision (loss of peripheral vision)
- disinhibition of spinal reflexes and shaking

After the fear event occurred, the amygdalae and hippocampus (memory area of the brain) record the event through nerve connection plasticity. The stimulation to the hippocampus will cause the individual to remember many details surrounding the situation.

Plasticity and memory formation in the amygdala are generated by activation of the neurons in the region. Experimental data supports nerve connections' (synaptic) plasticity of the neurons leading to the lateral amygdalae that occurs with fear conditioning.

Nerve plasticity or neuroplasticity is the ability of nerve (neuronal) networks in the brain to change through growth and reorganization. These changes range from individual nerve pathways making new connections to systematic adjustments like cortical remapping. Examples of neuroplasticity include circuit and network changes that result from learning a new ability, environmental influences, practice, and psychological stress.

In some cases, this memory plasticity forms permanent fear responses such as post-traumatic stress disorder (PTSD) or a phobia. Functional magnetic resonance imaging (fMRI) scans have shown that the amygdalae in individuals diagnosed with such disorders, including panic attacks, are larger and wired for a higher level of fear.

Once the person is in safe mode, meaning that there are no longer any potential threats surrounding them, the amygdalae will send this information to the medial prefrontal cortex (mPFC) where it is stored for similar future situations, which is known as memory consolidation. When the person or animal becomes calm, the parasympathetic nervous system is activated.

BIOLOGICAL MECHANISMS IN ANGER AND FEAR

The fight-and-flight responses have assumed a wider range of behaviors. For example, the fight response may be manifested in angry, argumentative behavior, and the flight response may be manifested through social withdrawal, substance abuse, or even social media.

The biological mechanisms of fear are multifactorial and complex. Fear is divided into mobility/avoidance (fight-or-flight response) and immobilization. The decision as to which particular fear behavior is performed is determined by the level of fear, type of threat of fear, and specific context.

Fear is considered a preparedness phenomenon. It can also be considered part of natural selection, whereby the fittest survive in response to danger. This is found in humans and animals. A weak caribou in Alaska cannot survive a wolf pack—even though fear is causing the caribou to try to escape death. The same is true for humans. When the danger is overpowering, fear cannot save a person. Although genetics can play a role in escaping or overcoming danger with fear, depending on the extent of the dangerous threat, survival cannot be ensured.

Perceived danger occurs in humans and animals. Perceived danger in humans is called anxiety. The same is true for animals. Hoofed animals stampede during thunder and lightning storms without knowing there is no imminent danger. I had a German shorthair dog that feared thunder. While at work, a thunderstorm would occur, and when I came home, the back door would be torn apart from her attempted escape. Her perception was that the thunder was in the house, and she was trying to run away from the storm. This perceived fear is also seen in animals during fireworks on the Fourth of July.

Fear is always linked to the sympathetic response, but it does not necessarily be a fight-or-flight response. Other factors can regulate the response, including knowledge and mindfulness. The executive part of the brain (prefrontal lobe) can regulate the response. For example, meeting a grizzly bear on a path while hiking would cause panic and flight. That could cause disaster. Staying still and looking the grizzly in the eyes, most likely will cause the bear to go in a separate direction. People who have encountered a great white shark have hit the shark on its snout, causing it to retreat. Fear can also cause a freeze response or paralysis.

Situations that are uncertain and unpredictable can cause anxiety. This unpredictable fear can be perceived as rational in war, terrorism, and totalitarian political systems. This is a result of persistent danger and terror. This type of anxiety can be perceived as rational.

A 2005 US. Gallup Poll sampled nearly one thousand teenagers (13-17 year old) as to what they feared the most as an open-ended question. The U.S. adolescents reported their top ten fearsas follows: terrorism attacks, spiders, death, failure, war, criminal or gang violence, being alone, the future, and nuclear war. If repeated in 2021, global warming would be added to the list. In a 2008 online survey, they were asked to provide their top fears. The assumption was that people online tend to seek information on the issues that concern them the most. The result indicated the most fears in the online survey were flying, heights, clowns, death, intimacy, refection, people, snakes, failure, and driving. These fears are real and rational, in that people have had experienced the cause of the fear or observed these fears themselves through the media.

Irrational fear can be learned early in life. Fear can be learned by experiencing or watching a traumatic accident. Learned fears occur at a young age as babies and toddlers or preschoolers. A large dog can cause ongoing fear to be afraid of any dogs—even into adulthood. A toddler falling into a deep ditch can cause a fear of heights. Threatening experiences can lead to irrational fears and phobias in adulthood. Phobias are an extreme or irrational fear of or aversion to something. Phobias include fear of large groups of people (enochlophobia), fear of heights (acrophobia), fear of enclosed spaces (claustrophobia), or fear of water (aqua phobia). Also, abuse as a child can lead to post-traumatic stress disorder.

Males and females tend to deal with stressful situations differently. Males are more likely to respond to an emergency situation with aggression (fight), and females are more likely to flee (flight), turn to others for help, or attempt to defuse the situation (tend and befriend). During stressful times, a mother is especially likely to show protective responses toward her offspring.

Fear of death is common in all cultures. To deal with fear of death, most cultures have rituals. These rituals help preserve cultural ideas. Many of these rituals are associated with cultural religions and show how living a peaceful and honorable life within the confines of God will determine life after death.

The greatest pronouncement of fear is religion. It promotes it in several forms: indoctrination, manipulation, contagious, mythology, and politics.

Christianity, compared to Buddhism, is a huge fearmongering religion. Indoctrination is the earliest form of creating fear in children. They say, "You must join the church to be saved by God." This psychological fear creates financial revenue and suggests all sins will be forgiven. This is all a part of the manipulation required to be a social member of the church. As part of this manipulation, they say, "By being a member of our church, God will save and find a place in heaven when you die."

The contagious promotion of fear occurs when members of the church reach out to save those who have not been saved by God. Seventh-day Adventists go from house to house to instill guilt in those who have not been saved. This creates long-term fears and anxiety. Much of this instilled fear is mythological.

Religion is an excellent portal for learning fear. Every step from cradle to death instills psychological fears. Being a good Christian allows one to have no fears of death. When a person sins, they fear death.

Fear in religion—associated with politics and the infiltration of government—dates back to the origins of the Catholic Church. The first Christian Church, according to the Bible, was at the time of Jesus in Jerusalem. The first organized Christian Church, was the Roman Catholic Church, began in the first three centuries CE. Roman Catholicism originated with the very beginnings of Christianity.

In 380 CE, under Emperor Theodosius, Christianity became the state religion of the Roman Empire. The Edict of Thessalonica, a decree of the emperor, claimed it would persist until the fall of the Western Roman Empire. After the fall of the Western Roman Empire in 476, the Catholic Church became a powerful social and political institution, and its influence spread throughout Europe.

GRIEF, FORGIVENESS, ACCEPTANCE, AND REJECTION

The pope became king of some kingdoms. The pope was the Holy Roman emperor, and bishops were responsible for elections.

In 1095, Pope Urban II made the most influential speech of the Middle Ages, giving rise to the Crusades. He called on all Christians in Europe to war against Muslims in order to reclaim the Holy Land and cry, "God wills it!"

The Battle of White Mountain (1620) in Bohemia was one of the decisive battles of the Thirty Years' War, which ultimately led to the forced conversion of the Bohemian population back to Roman Catholicism.

The European wars of religion were waged in Europe during the sixteenth, seventeenth, and early eighteenth centuries. After the Protestant Reformation began in 1517, the wars disrupted the religious and political order of Catholic countries in Europe. Nevertheless, Catholicism continues to play a role in politics to this day.

The Catholic Church's role in politics is by far the nation's longest-standing religious political influence. Evangelicals and Christian nationalism have also had influence, especially in the twenty-first century. Religion in politics creates fear in those who are victims as well as members of political religion.

Evolutionary psychologists believe fears, like fear of heights, are related to mammals that developed during the Mesozoic Era. That is overstated since monkeys have no fear of heights, and dolphins dive deep in the ocean. Fear is present in all mammals, birds, fish, and other marine life. Fear appears to be more innate than evolutionary. The evolutionary aspect of fear is prevention of harm. Camouflage to prevent harm to an organism is evolutionary. Fish and marine life are camouflaged in rocks, sand, and marine plants to keep them safe from predators. These creatures cannot fight or flee. An example is bottom fish, like flounder, that blends into its environment. There are many examples, but an excellent evolutionary example is the cuttlefish. This creature uses its ability to camouflage to attract prey and hide from predators. With the skill of changing color, shape, and texture, they are very good at blending into their surroundings. They could look like other fish, rocks, plants, and sand.

Emotions involved with Anger and crying:

The emotions that cause angry crying consist of hurt, betrayal, unjust treatment, and being attacked. It may be evolutionary that signals can summon help and distress. The act of crying causes release of oxytocin and endorphins, which leads to a calming effect.

Crying usually occurs in immediate adverse events. In anger and fear crying, the hypothalamus-pituitary-adrenal axis is activated in the brain. Fear and anger (stress) activate the amygdala. After the amygdala sends a distress signal, the hypothalamus activates the sympathetic nervous system by sending signals through the autonomic nerves to the adrenal glands. These glands respond by pumping the hormone epinephrine (also known as adrenaline) into the bloodstream.

Cortisol also regulates the hypothalamus-pituitary-adrenal (HPA) axis. When high amounts of cortisol interact with the hypothalamus, the HPA axis will slow down its activity. This allows for the prefrontal cortex to regulate our reactions to stress. It may also allow for the crying hormones and neurochemicals to take effect.

Fear can cause shrieking, screaming of crying—or all at the same time. Shrieking usually refers to a sharper and briefer cry than a scream. When caused by fear or pain, it is often indicative of more terror or distress. A scream is a long ear-piercing cry. Its causes are the same as with a shriek. Shrieks and screams can also be associated with joy and excitement. Hearing a scream, shriek, or cry triggers fear in the amygdala. This activates the sympathetic nervous system in the fight-or-flight response.

EMOTIONS INVOLVED WITH FEAR AND CRYING

Several triggers of fear are not rational, but they are not as extreme as phobias. According to surveys, some of the most common fears are evil powers, snakes, spiders, cockroaches, heights, Great White sharks, water, enclosed spaces, tunnels, bridges, needles, social rejection, and public speaking.

Social relations and culture can determine how a person responds to fear.

THE BIOLOGICAL PHYSIOLOGY OF CALMING AND SOOTHING

The autonomic nervous system is made up of the sympathetic nervous system and the parasympathetic nervous system. The sympathetic system, as noted above, is associated with the fight-or-flight response. Calming and soothing effects arise from the parasympathetic nervous system.

PARASYMPATHETIC NERVOUS SYSTEM

The parasympathetic nervous system is functionally opposite to the sympathetic nervous system. The parasympathetic nervous system (PSNS) is involved in relaxation and normal automatic functions of the body, such as heart rate, blood pressure, and digestion. The sympathetic nervous system (SNS) is involved with survival functions, such as fight-or-flight functions. The PSNS and SNS are both integrated in the hypothalamus, which is located just above the midbrain of the brain stem. The parasympathetic and sympathetic nervous systems are considered the two divisions of the autonomic nervous system.

The PSNS starts in the brain and extends out via long fibers that connect with special nerves (neurons) to the brain stem and down the spinal cord to ganglia that send out nerves near to the organ they intend to act on. Once PSNS signals hit these neurons, they have a short distance to travel to their respective organs.

AREAS THE PARASYMPATHETIC NERVOUS SYSTEM (PSNS) ACTS ON

eyes (constrict pupils)
lacrimal glands (produce tears)
parotid glands (produce saliva)
salivary glands (produce saliva)
nerves in the stomach and trunk (increase digestion)
nerves that go to the bladder (constricts the bladder)
nerves and blood vessels (responsible for the male erection)
decrease heart rate
tighten bronchi (breathing tubes in the lungs)
inhibit sympathetic nervous system neurotransmitters (adrenaline and noradrenaline)

The PSNS keeps the basic functions of the body working normally. It basically undoes the work of sympathetic division after stressful situations.

The neurotransmitters in the sympathetic nervous system are epinephrine and norepinephrine; in the parasympathetic nervous system, the neurotransmitters is acetylcholine (ACh), and peptides (such as cholecystokinin) may act on the PSNS.

ACh acts on two types of receptors, the muscarinic and nicotinic cholinergic receptors, and most transmission occurs in two stages. When stimulated, the preganglionic nerve releases ACh at the ganglion, which acts on nicotinic receptors of the postganglionic neurons. The postganglionic nerve then releases ACh to stimulate the muscarinic receptors of the target organ, such as the heart.

BIOLOGICAL MECHANISMS IN STRESS AND ANXIETY

Stress and anxiety are activated to some degree by the sympathetic nervous system. There are varying degrees of stimulation. Some are acute or immediate, and some chronic or long-acting, depending on the emotions involved.

Stress and anxiety often occur together, but these terms are not interchangeable. Even though symptoms commonly overlap, a person's experience with these emotions differs based on context. Stress is emotional tension that results from adverse or demanding circumstances. Stress relates to a known or understood adversity, and anxiety follows from an unknown, unexpected, or poorly defined threat. The different responses between the two is a result of one's emotional perception of various stressors. For example, a person with social anxiety will activate the sympathetic stress response (fight-or-flight response) in a crowd. Another person may feel stress from an adversarial boss, which generates a different sympathetic stress response.

Stress, unlike anxiety, is a result of external events producing the emotional sympathetic response. Stress can be positive or negative. Working on a very important project at work can produce a positive feeling of stress. However, worrying about if something will interfere with completion or whether it can be accomplished will cause anxiety. The anxiety will occur away from work—when not engaged in the project.

Anxiety is the result of internal tensions. It is a feeling of worry or dread that is not a direct reaction to a specific external cause with physical changes like increased heart rate and blood pressure.

In the previous example, there is uncertainty or worry about what the future holds. There is nothing tangible to the fear. Anxiety disorder is diagnosed when there are chronic or periodic experiences of anxiety, which are markedly out of proportion to current situations.

Anxiety can be normal (rational, short-term, and episodic anxiety) or abnormal (irrational, long-term, or persistent anxiety). These are called anxiety disorders. In a normal setting, the difference between concern and worry is relevant. Concern is having a specific connection to or responsibility to an interest or ability to do something. Worry is a state of uncertainty over an actual or potential problem. A mother can have concern about sending her child to school after a school shooting in the United States, but she cannot do anything in terms of her own situation, which leads to worry and anxiety.

This is a normal, rational form of anxiety. The associated physical symptoms are mild. The mother may have trouble concentrating or thinking about anything other than her present worry. She may develop muscle tension or tightness, especially around the neck and shoulders.

Physicians frequently see something called "white coat syndrome." The patient is seen by the doctor, and when taking the blood pressure, the pressure is extremely high. After talking to the doctor, the blood pressure is repeated and found to be normal. In this situation, the patient is nervous when coming to the doctor's office. Their blood pressure increased with their anxiety, and it returns to normal after they relax. This is considered a normal anxiety reaction.

Occasional anxiety is a normal part of life. However, people with anxiety disorders frequently have intense, excessive, and persistent worries and fears about everyday situations. Anxiety disorders often involve repeated episodes of sudden feelings of intense anxiety and fear or terror that reach a peak within minutes. These are called panic attacks. Anxiety disorders consist of several types of anxiety that are abnormal (irrational, long-term, or persistent) mental disorders.

SYMPTOMS OF ANXIETY

feeling of impending harm to oneself or to someone close
feeling like one is going to die
feeling mentally ill
feelings of urgency
trouble concentrating or thinking about anything other than the present worry
muscle tension or tightness (in women, usually around the neck and shoulders)
abnormal or excessive sweating
feeling flushed, hot, or cold
dry mouth
increased heart rate and/or blood pressure

fatigue
faint
sleeping disturbance or loss of sleep
rapid breathing (hyperventilating) or shortness of breath
headaches
dizziness, fainting, trembling
crying
avoidance of issues that trigger anxiety or panic

TYPES OF ANXIETY DISORDERS

Generalized anxiety disorder (GAD). This includes persistent and excessive anxiety and worry about activities or events—even ordinary, routine issues. The worry is out of proportion to the actual circumstance, is difficult to control, and affects how you feel physically. It often occurs along with other anxiety disorders or depression.

Panic disorder/attacks (PA). Panic attacks are repeated episodes of sudden feelings of intense anxiety and fear or terror that reach a peak within minutes. This is associated with an acute sympathetic response, including feelings of impending doom, shortness of breath, chest pain, or a rapid, fluttering, or pounding heart (heart palpitations). Panic attacks may lead to worrying about them happening again or avoiding situations in which they have occurred.

Phobias. Phobias are an intense, irrational fear of certain situations or objects that are unlikely to harm a person. Some of these fears may make sense, such as a fear of snakes, but the level of fear often does not match the situation. Phobia comes from the Greek word *phobos*, which means *fear* or *horror*. Phobias are different than regular fears because they cause significant distress, possibly interfering with life at home, work, or school. People with phobias actively avoid the phobic object or situation or endure it with intense fear or anxiety. There are many specific phobias, but common ones include fear of water (hydrophobia), fear of darkness (achluophobia), fear of heights (acrophobia), fear of flying (aerophobia), and fear of pain (ergophobia).

Social anxiety disorder. In the past, social anxiety was called social phobia. A person may have overwhelming worry and self-consciousness with daily social situations. A person may worry about others judging them. They may be anxious about being open to ridicule. People with social anxiety disorder may avoid social situations entirely.

Agoraphobia. People with agoraphobia may have an intense fear of enclosed spaces, lines or crowds, open spaces, or places outside of their home.

Separation anxiety: This condition mostly happens to children or teens, who may worry about being away from their parents. Children with separation anxiety disorder may fear that their parents will be hurt in some way or not come back as promised. It happens a lot to preschoolers, but older children and adults who have experienced a stressful event may have separation anxiety disorder as well. Loss of a family member or abandonment are the likely causes. Separation anxiety can also occur in military families.

Anxiety disorders are the most common mental health condition in the United States. They affect about forty million Americans. They happen to nearly 30 percent of adults at some point. Anxiety disorders most often begin in childhood, adolescence, or early adulthood.

If stress or anxiety are activated for too long, catecholamines (epinephrine and norepinephrine) can produce negative health effects. To counteract these negative effects, it's important to learn to return the body to its pre-stressed state. The body must be in a relaxed state to function normally.

After stress and anxiety are relieved—with no further sympathetic stimulation—the parasympathetic nervous system is activated to relieve the stress and anxiety, causing relaxation and normal organ and tissue function.

CRYING IN STRESS AND ANXIETY

Researchers have found that crying has a soothing effect; self-soothing is when people regulate their own emotions, and it helps them calm themselves. It reduces distress, stress, and anxiety. Crying can also help people get support from others around them.

When humans cry in response to stress, their tears contain a number of stress hormones and chemicals, such as catecholamines. Researchers believe that crying can reduce the levels of these chemicals in the body, which could reduce stress and anxiety.

Stress tightens muscles and heightens tension, and crying releases some of that that tension and controls muscle spasms. Crying activates the parasympathetic nervous system (PNS), which helps people relax, and relieves tension.

Crying helps a person with stress or anxiety to sleep. Babies cry themselves to sleep, and adults with stress or anxiety can improve their sleep when shedding tears at bedtime.

Anxiety can cause a person to cry. Symptoms of anxiety include worrying. Crying can help relieve stress.

GRIEF AND CRYING

Crying can help in the healing process of grief. Those who do not or cannot cry when they lose someone they love or have some other cause of grief often are much more vulnerable to depression and other health problems.

When people hold back their tears, it can lead to mental and physical problems. It takes a lot of effort to hold back tears. This often leads to depression.

Most people feel much better after a good cry, but their sense of catharsis depends partly on where and with whom the crying occurs. Person suffering from grief prefer crying alone and privately, but a sympathetic friend or family member could be supportive of them. When a grieving person cries in front of two or more people—for example, in the workplace or among strangers—the grieving crying person is less likely to get that intimate support and is more likely to be embarrassed.

Another advantage to crying during grief is that it can provide new insights into their suffering. For example, if the grieving person cannot be with the person who is gone, they can be comforted by memories.

Grief is also associated with sadness and depression, and it is one of the stages of the grieving process. Dr. Elizabeth Kübler-Ross wrote about the five stages of grief, and depression was one stage. This is essentially an adjustment disorder, that is usually a stage that does not last like chronic depression. The sadness and crying with grief are different from that of chronic depression.

Grief and the other stages lasts between six months and four years, and sadness with crying can appear intermittently. One study found that intense grief-related feelings peaked at about four to six months and gradually declined over the next two years.

SADNESS AND DEPRESSION AND CRYING

Sadness. Feeling sad, showing sorrow; unhappiness; caused by or characterized by sorrow, and regret; unfortunate or regrettable situations.

Depression. A feeling of disturbed surprise resulting from an upsetting event. A feeling of severe dependency and rejection. Depression is often accompanied by loss of energy, loss of appetite, and extended sleep. Sadness can be incorporated into depression, but not vice versa. Sadness is a short-lived feeling that does not have all the features of depression.

FEATURES OF SEVERE DEPRESSION

feelings of emptiness or hopelessness
angry outbursts, irritability, or frustration (even over small matters)
loss of interest or pleasure in most or all normal activities, such as sex, hobbies, or sports
sleep disturbances or sleeping too much
tiredness and lack of energy (even small tasks take extra effort)
reduced appetite and weight loss or increased cravings for food and weight gain
slowed thinking, speaking, or body movements
feelings of worthlessness or guilt, fixating on past failures or self-blame
trouble thinking, concentrating, making decisions, or remembering things
frequent or recurrent thoughts of death, suicidal thoughts, suicide attempts, or suicide
unexplained physical problems, such as back pain or headaches

These symptoms can develop in severe grieving situations.

Depression can be temporary or seasonal. When there is more daylight, the brain makes more serotonin, which prevents depression. Shorter days and longer hours of darkness in the fall and winter (especially in the far north) may lead the body to have more melatonin and less serotonin, leading to seasonal depression.

The most severe form of depression is major depressive disorder.

Research suggests that depression doesn't spring from simply having too much or too little of certain brain chemicals. Rather, there are many possible causes of depression, including faulty mood regulation by the brain, genetic vulnerability, stressful life events, medications, and medical problems.

In the twenty-first century, the most common causes of depression are continuing difficulties—long-term unemployment, abusive or uncaring relationships, long-term isolation or loneliness, prolonged work stress, prolonged unemployment, loss of secure living situations, financially poor or poverty—that are more likely to cause depression than recent life stresses.

Frequent crying can be a sign of depression. People may be depressed if their crying, :happens very frequently, happens for no apparent reason, starts to affect daily activities, or becomes uncontrollable

A frequent form of crying in sadness and depression is weeping. Weeping is like crying, by simply the shedding of tears, but sobbing is considered noisy crying.

HAPPINESS AND CRYING

Research has shown that tears of joy are associated with positive feelings. There are many theories about crying and what causes it, but the previous descriptions of crying are all related to emotions. Much of what has thus far been described has been the negative aspects of crying related to grief, stress, anger, and depression, but crying can also occur with positive emotions, such as joy and happiness. The fact that crying occurs with positive emotions debunks all theories unrelated to emotions and crying.

We have all witnessed a mother or a father shedding tears at a child's wedding. The emotion in part is sorrow that their children are leaving them—and the happiness of the celebration and that their son or daughter is forming a family.

We have witnessed Olympic gymnasts winning gold medals with perfect scores and shedding tears at the celebration. These are tears of hard work and stress relief and joy. I call this co-emotional or multifactorial emotional crying.

In 2021 Garth Brooks shed tears at the Kennedy Center for Performing Arts Awards when he was celebrated for his country music. Those were likely tears of joy and celebration. His tears occurred when other performing artists were singing songs he had written and performed. There is an argument that strong emotions like joy or sadness communicate socially that the tearful or crying person is in need of support or comfort. No one in the audience could see Garth's tears, and we would have not known if the TV camera had not shown his tears. Tears of joy do not necessarily require comfort or support from others. It is a personal emotional experience, independent of comfort or support, but if support occurs, it signifies an added emotion.

For dimorphous expression, a mother might be hugging her daughter and crying at the same time because the daughter kicked the winning goal for her soccer team.

Tears of joy may occur after a sexual orgasm. The endorphin-oxytocin-endocannabinoid triad takes place—along with sympathetic stimulus—in an orgasm. There is an overwhelming good feeling associated with the triad, and the person's heart rate increases along with flushing of the skin. The experience may be overwhelming joy that can create tears.

As we have learned with the biology of crying, the brain releases endorphins and oxytocin. These hormones can help relieve pain, boost mood, and improve general well-being. When a person cries with happiness, the oxytocin, endorphins, and social support can magnify the experience and make them feel even better—and maybe cry a little more.

It is important to note that the biological mechanism of crying remains the same, but the emotional stimulus is more complex with numerous emotional stimuli. Again, this shows how emotions play a significant role in the shedding of tears and crying.

A difference between negative and positive crying is that crying with joy occurs in both genders with the same frequency. It occurs with the same frequency in all ages.

SUMMARY

There are many propositions and theories about negative and positive crying. Negative and positive crying were explained as special and as public-private theories. None of these psychological proposals are logical or reasonable explanations of positive and negative crying.

One of the tears of joy theories is that the brain cannot distinguish the difference between the negative and positive emotions associated with crying. It postulates the hypothalamus, a part of the limbic system, responds to emotions through strong neural signals from the amygdala, which cannot always discern the difference between happy and sad signals. This theory states that only the limbic system is involved with happy or sad tears. It excludes all other parts of the central nervous system. A large part of sad and happy tears is our senses and experiences. Sight and memory play huge parts.

Another proposed theory is that crying is a social cue that broadly means "do not attack me—and consider appeasing me." This suggest that the person is in immediate need of close relationships, friends, or family. The crying person is submissive. This explanation is supposed to make sense for both sad and happy crying situations because it is biology's way of tearing down barriers and facilitating bonding. This psychological proposal makes some sense with crying in grief and sadness—but not in happy crying. Happy tears are not social; they are personal and independent. This proposal does not explain crying alone.

One of the most important sections in this chapter is the biological mechanisms that occur during crying. The parts of the brain involved with crying are the hypothalamus, amygdala, hippocampus, and parts of the midbrain. The neurotransmitters involved are endorphins, oxytocin, endocannabinoids, epinephrine, and norepinephrine. None of these—in the form of the limbic system—functions alone. The parts of the brain when crying are connected to the senses parts of the brain, such as vision or hearing, which trigger the emotions in the brain.

This system relies on stimuli or triggers to go through the process of forming tears and crying. These triggers include frustration, anger, fear, stress, sadness, grief, depression, anxiety, joy, and happiness. With all of the emotional stimuli, the end result is that the person feels better after the crying episode, which allows the parasympathetic nervous system to extend feelings of calm and emotional relaxation. This whole crying process is biologically and psychologically logical. It requires no theories.

Psychological tears and crying are a product of emotional sensory perception. Crying is considered normal. It does not signify weakness.

Many songs have been written with crying in the lyrics, including "Don't cry me a river. Don't cry me a river;

Because I'm crying a river over you "No tears left to cry

To:

Big girls don't cry!" Studies have shown that sad music leads to crying more than any other type of music.

Do not stop anyone from crying—and don't let anyone stop you from crying—because crying is the best release of emotions. It is positive and therapeutic.

CHAPTER 2
GRIEF

"Suffering, pain, and grief are inevitable. Suicide is not!"
Dr. Daniel Brubaker

Grief emotions and the stages thereof should be considered in accordance with the specific loss situation. The grief stages are much different from those of a person who experiences the loss of a loved one, which is different from a person with a chronic debilitating disease.

The stages of grief were first described in 1969 by Elisabeth Kübler-Ross, a Swiss-American psychiatrist, in *On Death and Dying*. Her work and book were inspired by her work with terminally ill patients. Motivated by the lack of instruction in medical schools on the subject of death and dying, Kübler-Ross examined death and those faced with it at the University of Chicago's medical school. Kübler-Ross's project evolved into a series of seminars, which, along with patient interviews and previous research, became the foundation of her book. Kübler-Ross's work was welcomed by all in medicine because there was no guide for physicians to deal with dying patients. As students in medicine, we all had to read her book.

THE FIVE STAGES OF GRIEF

DENIAL

The first reaction is denial. In this stage, individuals believe the diagnosis is somehow mistaken, and they cling to a false, preferable reality.

ANGER

When the individual recognizes that denial cannot continue, they become frustrated, especially at proximate individuals:

Why me? It's not fair!
How can this happen to me?
Who is to blame?
Why would this happen?

BARGAINING

The third stage involves the hope that the individual can avoid the cause of grief. Usually, the negotiation for an extended life is made in exchange for a reformed lifestyle. People facing less serious trauma can bargain or seek compromise. Examples include a terminally ill person who "negotiates with God" to attend a daughter's wedding, attempt to bargain for more time to live in exchange for a reformed lifestyle, or saying, "If I could trade their life for mine."

DEPRESSION

During the fourth stage, the individual despairs at the recognition of their mortality. In this state, the individual may become silent, refuse visitors, or spend much of the time mournful and sullen:

I'm so sad. Why bother with anything?
I'm going to die soon. What's the point?
I miss my loved one. Why go on?

ACCEPTANCE

In this last stage, individuals embrace mortality, the inevitable future, or another tragic event:

It's going to be okay.
I can't fight it. I may as well prepare for it.

Subsequent psychologists and clinicians have been critical of Kübler-Ross's stages as not being applicable to grief or not present during grief. However, it must be realized that these stages were observed and analyzed in persons who knew they were in the process of dying (such as in hospice). Could these five stages be applied to other grieving processes (such as the loss of a loved one)?

In 2014, Kübler-Ross (posthumously) and David Kessler published *Grief and Grieving: Finding the Meaning if Grief through the Five Stages of Loss*, which covered all forms of grief using the five stages. Personal grief now covered everything from the loss of a job or income, major rejection, the end of a relationship or divorce, an infertility diagnosis, and even minor losses, such as a loss of insurance coverage.https://en.wikipedia.org/wiki/Five_stages_of_grief Kessler has also proposed "meaning" as a sixth stage of grief.

There have been additional stages added to the five by Kübler-Ross. Seven and as high as ten stages of grief have been proposed. We provide the seven stages here, but ten gets ridiculous.

The seven stages of grief are another popular model for explaining the many complicated experiences of loss:

Shock and denial. This is a state of disbelief and numbed feelings.

Pain and guilt. One may feel that the loss is unbearable, which makes other people's lives difficult because of the griever's feelings and needs.

Anger and bargaining. The griever may lash out, telling God or a higher power that the griever will do anything they ask if they'll only grant relief from these feelings.

Depression. This may be a period of isolation and loneliness during which one processes and reflects on the loss.

The upward turn. At this point, the stages of grief, like anger and pain, have died down, and the griever is left in a more calm and relaxed state.

Reconstruction and working through grief. One can begin to put the pieces of the griever's life back together and carry forward.

Acceptance and hope. This is a very gradual acceptance of the new way of life and a feeling of possibility in the future.

Grief is a feeling of deep sorrow that is found in all humans and other mammals. At some point in everyone's life, there will be at least one encounter with grief. It may be from the death of a loved one, the loss of a job, the end of a relationship, or a change in life that causes deep sorrow.

Grief is very personal, and it is unpredictable about when it occurs. One may cry, become angry, withdraw, or feel empty. None of these things are unusual or wrong. Everyone grieves differently, but there are some commonalities in the stages and the order of feelings experienced during grief.

The five stages by Kübler-Ross were very specific to dying patients who she empirically observed firsthand. Her observations and analysis are very specific to hospice patients. Her five stages also provided physicians, medical students, postgraduate physicians, and other health care providers a guide for dealing with dying patients.

The problems can become disorderly and unrealistic. Other forms of grief, such as a loss of a job, do not fit into the five stages, but a couple may fit.

TYPES OF GRIEF

Psychologists have designated multiple types of grief. These include delayed grief, distorted grief, cumulative grief, prolonged grief, exaggerated grief, marked grief, traumatic grief, collective grief, ambiguous grief, inhibited grief, abbreviated grief, and absent grief.

Delayed grief is grief symptoms that are delayed for a long period after the death or loss of a loved one. The person avoids the reality and pain of the loss.

Distorted grief is an extreme, intense, atypical reaction to loss. Anger and hostility occur with oneself or others.

Cumulative grief is when one experiences a second loss while still grieving a first loss. This is also grief overload.

Prolonged grief is considered chronic grief. It is incapacitating grief on a daily basis, and it lasts for a long time.

Exaggerated grief is an overwhelming intensification of normal grief reactions that may worsen over time.

Marked grief is grief symptoms that impair normal function without the person recognizing the symptoms, and the symptoms could be physical or emotional.

Disenfranchised grief occurs in cultures. Societies or groups can invalidate a person's grief resulting from a loss. They may evaluate suicide, HIV, or drunk-driving deaths as insignificant.

Traumatic grief is a result of a loved one dying in a way that is frightening, horrifying, unexpected, violent, and/or traumatic, usually causing impairment of daily functions.

Collective grief is felt by a group, a community, or even an entire country. A good example is the terror attack of September 11, 2001 in the United States. This is usually associated with the death of a group or a massive number of deaths.

Ambiguous grief is when the loss lacks clarity, which may affect the grieving symptoms.

Inhibited grief is when an individual shows no outward signs of grief for an extended period of time.

Abbreviated grief is a short-lived period of grieving symptoms. This is thought to be due to little attachment to the deceased person.

Absent grief is when an individual should show grief—but does not show any signs or symptoms of grief. This is also associated with extended periods of shock or denial.

These explanations compartmentalize grief, but they are not very helpful for helping grieving individuals. For example, inhibited grief is when the individual shows no signs of grief. If this is found in a person with a personality disorder, the label is not helpful. These labels may be helpful for treatment, but they may cause more problems if the individual is labeled. There are also several overlapping types, such as inhibited and absent grief. How does someone call this grief when there are no symptoms? It may be perceived as abnormal that the person is not grieving over the death of a family member, but there may not have been a close relationship between them. Marked and exaggerated grief are variations of the same theme.

LOGICAL AND PRACTICAL FORMS OF GRIEF

Grief is the constellation or spectrum of internal thoughts and feelings we have when someone we love dies. In other words, grief is the internal meaning given to the experience of loss. Mourning is when you take the grief you have on the inside and express it outside of yourself.

As a result of categorizing illogical stages for different grieving circumstances, and illogical types of grief, we categorize grief, not to stages or types, but to specific circumstances that trigger the grief process. Grief is a process, but it is not necessarily completed in stages. Grieving is universal, but different cultures go through different processes.

It seems more reasonable to place the grieving processes into acute and chronic grief. It is noted that it may take a person anywhere from six months to four years to accept the loss of a loved one.

In medicine, we usually define acute illness or injury as one that takes three to six months to heal or go away. Any disease or injury lasting longer is considered chronic. The same can be applied to grief.

Chronic grief can develop into a mental health disorder. This can be described as adjustment disorder with depression. Common symptoms of chronic grief include prolonged sadness on a daily basis and/or extreme focus on the loss.

One can correlate acute and chronic grief with pain. In fact, it can be part of the grieving process. Acute pain is associated with an injury or surgery and can last three to six months. Opioids are used to diminish pain; some persons who have high tolerance for pain may only take a narcotic for a few weeks, but a person with a pain low tolerance may require narcotics for a month or two. The adaptive process to physical pain can vary with individuals.

Grief should also be characterized according to primary and secondary persons affected. Primary grief occurs to a person directly. Secondary grief occurs with a person who has suffered a loss from someone or something closely associated with the person experiencing the loss. This allows for the degree or extent of grief associated with either person. Grief occurs with those primary persons affected and those who experience a loss from a close relationship to the secondary grieving person. We hear about the loss of life of many types in the media. We hear about someone who died in a motor vehicle accident, but we don't grieve unless it is someone we know well.

ACUTE GRIEF

Acute grief is also called normal grief by some psychologists. However, we do not call this normal grief because of the multifactorial grieving process. Acute grief occurs in the early period after a loss, and it usually dominates the life of a bereaved person for between three and six months. The emotional reactions depend on the type of loss and how close the deceased person was to the person who is grieving.

Adapting and coping also depend on the general positivity or negativity of the person. Does the person see the glass as half full or half empty? The psychological makeup or mental health of the grieving person is another factor. The grieving process varies from individual to individual and is unpredictable. However, acute or normal grief is marked by movement toward acceptance of the loss, a gradual alleviation of the symptoms, and the ability to continue to engage in basic daily activities. The acceptance should take place within six months.

Consideration must be taken into account as to whether the loss primarily involves the individual or is secondary in terms of a person having a loss of someone or something closely associated to them. This distinction is very important in the acute phase of grief.

Acute grief is a complex, multifaceted experience that is often powerful and disruptive. Our initial reaction is to try to protect ourselves from the unwanted consequences of the loss of something to ourselves or a loss of someone close to us. The best ways to show these multifaceted emotions are through multiple examples.

However, common emotions throughout different example are mental pain or anguish and crying.

Acute primary loss causes many emotions related to grief, depending on the type of loss. There are many different types of loss. The loss of a job can affect persons in different ways. A narcissist who is terminated from a job may not have any grief. A person with paranoia may say, "I knew they didn't like my work or me as a person." These persons may be sad and depressed from the loss. The method of termination from a job can determine the grieving process.

If a mentally healthy individual is terminated without reason, the person may be shocked, cry with anger, become sad with crying, or feel anxious as they try to figure out the situation. Depression may set in during the healing process. As the person mentally heals from the loss, and as the grieving process comes to a close (acceptance), the person may form a future plan, which could mean finding a job with a different employer in the same business, returning to school to take a different direction in employment, or forming their own business. This process usually lasts less than a week and up to three months, which makes it acute. Dependent factors are friends, family, and partners who provide advice and support.

A person terminated with reason may be initially angry, may or may not cry, and may initially have denial, but after some thought, they will begin to understand that their problem requires change and acceptance. This may lead to being a better employee at another employer. One can apply different scenarios to the personal loss, and most all cause some form of grieving. However, it is important to recognize that none of these follow Elizabeth Kübler-Ross's five stages of grief: denial, anger, bargaining, depression, and acceptance.

The loss of a farm or business can lead to several stages of grief. The person trying to hang on to the farm or business might see the inevitable happening. The circumstances might provide different grief responses. If the situation for the farmer or business is a result of the government imposing tariffs or the loss of shipping resources, the grieving response might be anger, because of losing relationships and resources for purchasing and shipping goods. Anxiety may set in along with depression—for healing and resting the brain—and bargaining may set in. The farmer might contact their congressmen and ask for help since they were the cause of their demise.

Losing a farm to bankruptcy or other business due to global warming or other environmental conditions can cause significant grief. If years of drought or flooding cause a loss of income or bankruptcy, grief might set in.

The grieving response depends on circumstances surrounding the loss. Anxiety may occur in some persons, which may lead to them contacting the United States Department of Agriculture to find what they can plant to provide an income for their families. Others might be about to lose their farms or businesses to bankruptcy. This may lead to anger and denial. They might ask, "How can this be happening to me? It may lead to bargaining with the bank or the government. With religious persons, it may lead to bargaining with God. Crying may occur in all the stages of grief, especially if someone is losing a hundred-year-old farm or business. Depression may occur. This could go in two directions. It could provide a healing process with acceptance and future possibilities—or it could lead to suicide.

An acute secondary loss may be as simple as watching dead United States Military Men and Women who died in combat returned to their families. The acute secondary grief process is real.

An example of acute primary and secondary grieving persons can be found in certain divorces. When a spouse cheats on the other, they both might grieve in different ways. The person who cheated (primary person) may be in denial. They could be bargaining or feeling remorse, sadness, depression, or loneliness, especially if the person is totally abandoned by the person who he or she had the affair, plus the divorce. The person who was cheated on (secondary person) may feel betrayed, hurt, angry, and sad. These feelings may last six months, and depending on the circumstances, some of the feelings my occur intermittently over longer periods of time.

Should a married person decide they no longer want to be married, the secondary person may be shocked, dismayed, angry, lonely, or depressed. They might try to bargain, cry, or not accept what happened. The situation may linger.

Another example would be discovering a serious health problem, such as cancer. People experience different feelings and emotions. The first acute stages are shock, disbelief, and denial. Anxiety usually occurs until the final diagnosis and treatment. Persons with strong faith may turn everything over to God, which is a form of denial and acceptance. If the cancer has metastasized, the person may experience sadness, crying, bargaining, or depression. Grief is situational and does not necessarily follow Elizabeth Kübler-Ross's five stages.

I took a different direction when my cancer was discovered. Denial was the only stage of grief that took hold. All the signs and symptoms of colon cancer were denied, which made things worse. When the gastroenterologist performed the colonoscopy and found the cancer, he took pictures of the cancer. He showed me the pictures and asked me if I wanted them. I told him I wanted to take home the pictures and throw darts at them.

The surgeon removed the tumor, which was quite large and wrapped around my right kidney. The day after the surgery, he visited my hospital room and had a look of grief for me.

Chemotherapy was started, and instead of going through the stages of grief, I decided to ignore the diagnosis. Instead, I worked, rode mountain bikes, and went on with determination that the cancer would not interfere with my life.

It later metastasized to the right lobe of my liver. I told the oncologist to send me to someone who could remove the right lobe of the liver. That was done, and another year of chemotherapy went by. I continued to live my life as if I never had cancer. Twenty-two years went by with no cancer. The grief stages were not a part of the diagnosis—except for denial. People respond in different ways to a potential loss of life.

Many families have lost their homes in wildfires, floods, tornados, and hurricanes. Grief can occur in many different forms and stages. Denial and bargaining are not involved because the loss is swift and obvious. The immediate feelings are sadness, and there could be significant crying. Everything they owned including pictures, antiques or possession in the family for years are all gone. When thinking about memories, sadness and crying set in. Anger may also be felt, especially if a wildfire was started by humans. Depression and anxiety are to be expected. The length of these feelings depends upon support and recovery. Memories may cause intermittent crying episodes.

Acute secondary personal grief occurs when someone or something very close to the individual is permanently lost. It is expected that someone will grieve after the loss of a parent, sibling, partner, child, pet, or best friend. The feelings and emotional responses and coping processes vary between individuals and according to the situation or occurrence of the loved one's death.

The age of the grieving person is important. A child losing a mother or father is different from an adult losing a parent. A child or teenager may initially feel mental pain. This may last for some time. Many questions may arise about why they lost their parent. Crying will be a large part of their grief. The way the questions are answered by the surviving parent can play a role in the grief response. Anger, anxiety, loneliness, and sadness will all play a part in their grieving. The order is not important. Coping will depend on support from the surviving parent, relatives, and friends—and their own ability to mentally and physically cope. As they become adults, memories will always be there to create tears and sadness, but this does not interfere with their lives. Other children may fall into a chronic depressive disorder.

The circumstances of the loved one's death is a factor in how an individual responds to the loss. A sudden, unexpected death will likely cause immediate shock and a sense of loss with crying. A loved one who dies suddenly from a heart attack or injury creates a different grief response than one who dies slowly. A sudden death may cause immediate shock or withdrawal. Sadness with episodes of crying will occur early in the grieving process. If it is a spouse, loneliness, depression, and sexual bereavement can set in. Denial, anger, and bargaining do not seem to play a significant role in this situation. Sadness with crying episodes may occur periodically.

Many people are very close to their pets. A sudden loss—like getting killed or stolen—may initially lead to sadness and crying, especially with children. However, this loss may be accepted much more readily than with a human.

My son picked a German shorthair pointer dog out of a litter of pups and named her Arista. As the dog grew up, we jogged with her because she loved to run—it is in the breed. Arista became more attached to me as a result of caring for her and taking her for runs. In open areas where she could run free, she loved chasing sandpipers birds and pointing at butterflies.

Two years after surviving stage IV colon cancer, I went through a divorce and lost a child custody battle. As I went through the grieving process, Arista recognized every emotion and comforted me. Throughout the years, having different breeds of dogs, Arista was the most in tune with grief, especially crying. She eventually had to be put down due to cancer. She was cremated, and we still have her ashes. My wife, my son, and I experienced so much sadness after her death. I hung an oil painting of Arista, a gift from my wife, by my computer. Arista also loved my new wife. My wife and I still have memories of her. This periodic remembrance is called chronic intermittent uncomplicated grief. These brief moments of grief are a result of memories. An anniversary or a memory, which may cause tears, but they will not interfere with the normal functions of the person. This is also an example of secondary grief.

Gender affects a person's response to loss. Men do not show their grief as easily as women do. Males often view grief as more of a time to share activities than emotions. Women, on the other hand, tend to be more emotional and will work on their grief by talking about it. They may initially feel isolated, which allows them to accept the help of others. They will tell their story repeatedly because it helps them process and work through their grief.

Male roles tend to interfere with grieving. Typically, men and women grieve very differently, and it is helpful to understand the different patterns. Women may feel sadness, cry openly, and talk openly about their pain. Men may appear cold, irritable, angry, or depressed, and they often cannot talk easily about their pain.

Intuitive and instrumental grief are two ends of the grieving scale, which especially applies to gender grieving. Intuitive grieving is an internal experience that is characterized by extreme sadness and pain. The outward experience is characterized by emotional expression, such as crying. Intuitive grieving applies to females.

Instrumental grieving is an internal experience characterized by mental separation from the loss and an outward experience characterized by a lack of emotions.

These individuals utilize a cognitive, problem-solving approach and are more likely to direct their energy into activities. They perceive loss as a challenge to overcome. If any emotion is shown, anger is usually the most readily expressed feeling. Instrumental grieving tends to occur more frequently in men, but there is no clear line between the two. These two grieving styles may also be cultural.

Underlying personalities also play a role in how a person responds to loss. A person with a histrionic or obsessive personality might cry hysterically when they learn of the loss of someone close to them. A narcissistic or antisocial personality disorder person may not have any significant emotions. Coping skills will also vary.

The prolonged dying process of a loved one can cause different responses at the time of the loss. A person who is going through the prolonged sequence of dying will likely experience Elizabeth Kübler-Ross's five stages of grief: denial, anger, bargaining, depression, and acceptance. The secondary person with the dying loved one will likely experience the same stages as the dying loved one. Psychologists call this anticipatory grief. However, for the secondary person, confusion with feelings and guilt may also occur. After the loved one dies, there are no surprises. The person experiences sadness, crying, and temporary episodes of depression.

ADJUSTMENT DISORDER WITH DEPRESSION

According to Substance Abuse and Mental Health Services Administration (SAMHSA), the definition of adjustment disorder (AjD) is diagnosed when a person starts showing an excessive, extreme reaction to a stressful life event, such as the death of a loved one, a job loss, or divorce.

Adjustment disorder with depressed symptoms extend to problems functioning at an expected level in a job, learning environment, social setting, or other important area of functioning. Although considered a type of anxiety disorder, it manifests symptoms of depression, such as sadness, tears, and hopelessness. Being overwhelmed, withdrawing socially, experiencing a lack of pleasure in the things you used to enjoy interfere with normal daily activities.

Acute adjustment disorders usually have symptoms for up to six months, and chronic adjustment disorder lasts more than six months (until removal of the stressor or acceptance).

Adjustment disorder with depression is similar to grieving because both are triggered by a severe or significant loss or an identifiable life change, such as a move, job change, or divorce. It is different from a major depressive disorder because a major depressive disorder is not triggered by a loss. Adjustment disorder traditionally resolves within six months, and major depressive disorder tends to last much longer and can only be resolved with professional treatment.

Chronic adjustment disorder features symptoms longer than six months and causes major disruption in a person's life. As opposed to a major depressive disorder, this entity must be preceded by the acute adjustment disorder and must be associated with a life-changing experience. Many people erroneously think that adjustment disorder is less serious than other mental health disorders since it involves stress. Therefore, chronic adjustment disorder with depression is treated with psychotherapy, medications, and changes in life experiences, which is similar to treating major depressive disorders.

The symptoms of chronic adjustment disorders with depression are not that different from the symptoms of major depressive disorder. They include feelings of sadness, tearfulness, sleep disorders, hopelessness, irritability, loss of appetite, and withdrawal from normal activities. The only difference between acute and chronic is how long the symptoms last.

Chronic adjustment disorder with depression should not last more than two or three years (with or without treatment). At four years, it has developed into a major depressive disorder.

Major depressive disorder is a type of mental illness in which a person feels so sad that they are unable to function normally in everyday life. The symptoms are usually severe and may lead to suicide attempts. People with MDD often look very sad, and they often neglect their personal hygiene and eat poorly.

CHRONIC GRIEF

Chronic grief has symptoms that lasts more than six months—and the symptoms may last for years. According to sociological and psychological descriptions, chronic grief includes strong grief reactions that do not subside, and people experience extreme distress over the loss with no progress toward feeling better or improving functioning. This grief has also been labeled as prolonged grief, but this term offers no substantial information. It is associated with nonfunctional extreme symptomatic grief, but prolonged grief can be intermittent and functional.

Another term that is used for chronic grief is complicated grief. Complicated grief is like being in an ongoing, heightened state of mourning that keeps you from healing. Signs and symptoms of complicated grief may include intense sorrow, pain, and rumination over the loss of a loved one. These people can focus on little else but their loved one's death.

Chronic adjustment disorder should also be considered under chronic grief.

We have divided chronic grief into two categories: a benign, functional, healthy form of grief and one that is unhealthy, creating mental health issues.

CHRONIC INTERMITTENT FUNCTIONAL GRIEF

Mild grief symptoms—with or without tears—occur over a long period of time and are associated with memories of the loss of the loved one. This has also been called integrative grief. The person is completely functional, but there may be things that trigger their memories. The loss may be remembered during wedding anniversaries, anniversaries of their loss, or other events that bring back memories of the lost one. A good example is the survivors, friends, and family of loved ones lost during the September 11, 2001 terrorist attack on the United States World Trade Centers in NY, Pentagon, and plane crash near Pittsburgh. Every year, there is a national reminder, but loved ones also grieve at other times of the year. They function with jobs, activities, and family throughout the year, but episodes of grief occur. This is normal, but long lasting, which makes it chronic. Someone with chronic back pain doesn't have pain all of the time, but they have periodic flare-ups.

UNHEALTHY DYSFUNCTIONAL CHRONIC GRIEF

Chronic grief has been given different names by psychologists and sociologists. Chronic grief has several names that include prolonged grief, dysfunctional grief, complicated grief, complex grief disorder, persistent complex bereavement disorder, and prolonged grief disorder.

PROLONGED GRIEF

Prolonged grief has been defined as chronic grief. It is incapacitating grief on a daily basis, and it lasts for a long time. This term is descriptive and provides no benefit for categorization of grief. It is associated with long dysfunctional grief. However, the term suggests any grief lasting more than six months, including functional grief, such as chronic intermittent uncomplicated (functional) grief.

Prolonged grief has also been associated with complicated grief. The terminology can be confusing. Seeking a compromise between definitions of complicated and prolonged grief, the most recent *Diagnostic and Statistical Manual of Mental Disorders* (DSM-5) created yet another condition. Persistent complex bereavement disorder is listed in the appendix as a disorder that requires further study. However, there is no significant change in the confusion; in fact, it appears to have made chronic grief definitions worse.

DYSFUNCTIONAL GRIEF

Dysfunctional grieving represents a failure to follow the predictable course of normal grieving to resolution. It is a term that originated in the 1940s. When the process deviates from the norm, the individual becomes overwhelmed and resorts to maladaptive coping.

COMPLICATED GRIEF

Complicated grief (also referred to as complex grief disorder or persistent complex bereavement disorder) consists of long-lasting, severely painful emotions that prevent someone from recovering from the loss and resuming their life. It has more comprehensively been defined as a form of persistent, pervasive grief that does not get better naturally; it can occur when the natural thoughts, feelings, and behaviors that occur during acute grief gain a foothold and interfere with the ability to accept the reality of the loss.

Complicated grief is like being in an ongoing, heightened state of mourning that prevents someone from healing. In general, the signs and symptoms of complicated grief include intense sorrow, pain, and rumination over the loss of the loved one. They focus on little else but their loved one's death.

Different people follow different paths through the grieving experience. The order and timing of these phases may vary from person to person.

Signs and symptoms of complicated grief include intense sorrow, pain, and rumination over the loss of the loved one. There is little focus on anything other than the loved one's loss. There may be extended avoidance of or detachment of the loved one's reminders, such as holidays. There is intense and persistent longing for the deceased. Anger and bitterness often occur. The person may feel like life holds no meaning. They may be unable to enjoy life or think back on positive experiences with the loved one.

As the symptoms of grief become more severe, the person becomes more dysfunctional. The person becomes isolated from others and totally withdraws from social interaction. Severe complicated grief can lead to depression, deep sadness, guilt, and self-blame. The depression may develop into thoughts of suicide or wishing they had died with their loved one. Ultimately, there are problems accepting the death.

Complicated grief increases the risk of physical and mental health problems, including depression, anxiety, sleep issues, and physical illness. It's not known what causes complicated grief. As with many mental health disorders, it may involve environment, personality, inherited traits, and body's natural chemical makeup, such as hormones or lack thereof. There are risk factors in which some persons may be more prone to complicated grief.

Complicated grief occurs more often in females and older people. It is more common when the loved one dies unexpectedly from violence, homicide, or suicide or after the death of a child or a close dependent relationship, such as a disabled person losing the person who provides for their needs. If a person is socially isolated or lacks a support system, they are prone to complicated grief. Any prior history of mental health issues—such as depression, anxiety, or post-traumatic stress disorder—is also a risk factor. A person is also at risk after childhood trauma. Stressors that the person has difficulty managing, like financial difficulties, may also contribute.

Complicated grief is often treated with complicated grief therapy. It's similar to the psychotherapy techniques used for depression and PTSD, but it's specifically designed for complicated grief. This treatment can be effective when done individually or in a group format.

PROLONGED GRIEF DISORDER

Prolonged grief disorder (PGD) is a form of grief that is persistent and pervasive and interferes with functioning. It's characterized by persistent intense yearning, longing, and/or preoccupation with thoughts and memories of the person who died. Other symptoms include identity disruption, a marked sense of disbelief, avoidance of reminders of the loss, intense emotional pain related to the death, difficulty engaging in ongoing life, emotional numbness, feeling like life is meaningless, or intense loneliness. Prolonged grief continues to dominate a bereaved person's mind. The future seems bleak and empty, and the bereaved person feels lost and alone.

TERMINOLOGY ASSOCIATED WITH CHRONIC GRIEF

There is a lot of confusion about the terminology associated with grief. A simple way of describing acute and chronic grief is chronic functional grief and chronic unhealthy dysfunctional grief.

Acute grief lasts up to six months, and the grieving person becomes adapted to the loss in some way. During chronic grief, grieving can be functional, dysfunctional, or integrative for prolonged periods. All of these terms can apply to the acute stage, which is also referred to as normal grief.

Chronic grief is when grieving symptoms last more than six months. Chronic intermittent functional grief is also called integrative grief. This grief occurs intermittently over many years and is usually associated with memory.

The terminology for chronic unhealthy grief is very confusing, but the symptoms are all the same. As of 2021, there is no official diagnostic criteria for chronic grief.

OFFICIAL DIAGNOSTIC CRITERIA (FROM THE COMPLICATED GRIEF WEBSITE)

The most recent versions of the official diagnostic guidelines include a diagnosis of "prolonged grief disorder" in *Diagnostic and Statistical Manual of Mental Disorders* (DSM 5) and International Classification of Disease, eleventh version (ICD-11). This is the condition we have been calling complicated grief [2]:

In 2018, the World Health Organization approved a new diagnosis of prolonged grief disorder.

> A persistent and pervasive grief response characterized by longing for the deceased or persistent preoccupation with the deceased accompanied by intense emotional pain (e.g. sadness, guilt, anger, denial, blame, difficulty accepting the death, feeling one has lost a part of one's self, an inability to experience positive mood, emotional numbness, difficulty in engaging with social or other activities).

You can find the full guideline on the internet at ICD-11 for Mortality and Morbidity Statistics [2, 3].

In 2020, the American Psychiatric Association approved a new diagnosis of Prolonged Grief Disorder. The official announcement is pending. The criteria for this disorder are more specific, but our data and that of others confirm that they harmonize well. DSM-5 prolonged grief disorder requires the occurrence of a persistent and pervasive grief response characterized by persistent longing or yearning and/or preoccupation with the deceased accompanied by at least three of eight additional symptoms: disbelief, intense emotional pain, identity confusion, avoidance of reminders of the loss, feelings of numbness, intense loneliness, meaninglessness, or difficulty engaging in ongoing life.

Prolonged grief disorder (PGD) is often confused with depression. There is solid evidence that treatment for depression is far less helpful than targeted grief treatment, and this difference is important. Core symptoms of PGD are persistent yearning and preoccupation with the deceased, and the core symptoms of depression are pervasive, "free-floating" sadness and loss of interest and pleasure. These differences can help you distinguish grief from depression. Tens of millions of people worldwide are struggling with PGD.

Intense grief is typical after we lose someone close. Grief remains intense until we adapt to the loss. For an estimated 10–15 percent of bereaved people in the general population, adapting is problematic. Rates are higher when the death is sudden, unexpected, or violent or when a young person dies. Risk factors for PGD include a prior history of mood or anxiety disorders. Women are at higher risk than men. An estimated 20 percent of people receiving mental health treatment have unrecognized PGD.

BRAIN AND BODY CHEMISTRY ASSOCIATED WITH GRIEF

There is much to learn about the chemistry of grief because of all the different emotions associated with the grieving process. In general, this was covered under the first chapter on crying. The limbic system in the brain is involved. The sympathetic and parasympathetic systems are involved, especially when related to stress. All of this affects the body as loss of sleep or irregular sleep, loss of appetite, fatigue, migraines or headaches, lack of concentration, episodes of crying, and body aches and pains.

The main subcortical limbic brain regions implicated in depression are the amygdala, hippocampus, and dorsomedial thalamus. Both structural and functional abnormalities in these areas have been found in depression. Decreased hippocampal volumes (10, 25) have been noted in subjects with depression.

CULTURAL CUSTOMS FOR ADAPTATION TO GRIEF

Adapting to grief is influenced by cultural norms. The definition of culture includes the beliefs, values, behaviors, traditions, and rituals that members of a cultural group share.

Every culture has its own death rituals and customs. This helps people with the grieving process. Rituals provide grieving people and the community ways to process and express their grief. It allows the community to support the bereaved.

The cultural approach to funerals contrasts from a solemn, sad Christian funeral to a more celebratory African American funeral and a natural, celebratory Native American funeral, but all of them provide different rituals and cultural differences in the United States.

Christian funerals are usually a two-day process with a viewing of the embalmed body in a casket the night before the burial. On the day of the burial, a religious funeral service is held in the morning, followed by a luncheon, and the service usually reflects on the afterlife and the deceased person's life. The body is either buried in a casket in a graveyard or cremated with ashes placed in an urn.

African American funerals are different than white Protestant funerals, which leads to a different grieving process. African Americans express both sadness and exuberant joy in their celebrations of death. African Americans incorporate jazz, blues, and gospel songs in their funerals. These soulful events include songs of sadness and the promise of gladness in life everlasting.

Native American burials are an example of rituals associated with adapting to bereavement. There are 564 tribes in North America. Each tribe has its own traditional cultural custom. Each has its own language, symbols, ceremonial objects, and practices. Native people consider the natural world a sacred place, and religious activities are attached to specific places. Many also believe that birth, life, and death are part of an endless cycle.

The Shoshone-Bannock tribe in Idaho creates a tepee for the body to lie in honor for several days (in modern times, dry ice is placed in the casket) with a campfire burning outside. The body is in an oak, cedar, or pine casket. The body is never left alone during this time. Women feed visitors, and children help while being taught the etiquette of entering the tepee and other traditions. Some families dress the deceased in full regalia and jewelry, including moccasins for their trip to the next world [4].

Every family and tribe has its own traditional prayers, songs, smudging, and items that may be buried with the deceased. A medicine man may perform a ceremony in the tribe's native language. Many tribes restrict what bereaved relatives can eat and the activities they can engage in after the death of a loved one. The length of time for mourning varies by tribe [4].

Burial is natural, which is referred to as the green burial. Burial is in a wooden casket into rich ground. The body and wooden casket decompose naturally. Native Americans defend their burial grounds because they consider them sacred and respectful for the deceased.

These examples clearly show the differences in the format of funerals between cultures and racial groups. Rituals vary in so many ways in different cultures and races that one would expect varying rituals and custom associated with death and funerals. Different religions are a perfect example of different rituals and customs. There are two universal motifs in each funeral and grieving process: some form of religion and life after death.

SUMMARY

Grief is the constellation or spectrum of internal thoughts and feelings when there is primary grief (such as loss of job or divorce) or secondary grief (when someone we love dies). In other words, grief is the internal meaning given to the experience of loss. Mourning is when you take the grief you have on the inside and express it outside of yourself.

Grief occurs in stages—but not necessarily in any specific order. It is essential to be aware of these coping processes. Awareness of the severity is very useful in terms of seeking professional help.

REFERENCES

1. https://complicatedgrief.columbia.edu/professionals/complicated-grief-professionals/overview/
2. ICD-11 Prolonged Grief Disorder Criteria—NCBI
3. https://agoodgoodbye.com/religious-traditions/native-american-funeral-traditi

CHAPTER 3
FORGIVENESS

"Forgive and forget—sometimes is never met."
By: Dr. Daniel Brubaker

Forgiveness. The action or process of forgiving or being forgiven

Forgive. To stop feeling anger or resentment toward someone for an offense, flaw, or mistake. No longer feeling anger or wishing to punish a flaw, offense, or mistake.

Apologize. To express regret for something that one has done wrong.

Forgiving. Being ready and willing to forgive.

Apology. A regretful acknowledgment of an offense or failure.

Reconciliation. To relieve of a responsibility, obligation, or hardship or to clear from accusation or blame.

Vindication. The action of absolutely absolving someone from blame.

Forbearance. Patience, self-control, restraint, and tolerance.

RELIGIOUS VIEWS OF FORGIVENESS

Most religions incorporate forgiveness into their religious activities. It is done with religious dogma, teachings, affirmations, and activities. Although there are numerous religions, only a few representative religions are covered in their definition of forgiveness. We chose ancient religions and Abrahamic religions.

FORGIVENESS IN THE ANCIENT RELIGIONS—HINDUISM, JAINISM, AND BUDDHISM

HINDU DHARMA

Hinduism is the oldest religion recorded. Hinduism has approximately 1.35 billion adherents (15–16 percent of the world's population). The origins in India date back to prehistoric times known as Vedic religion between 10,000 BCE and 8,000 BCE. A transition between the Vedic religion and Hinduism took place between 800 and 200 BCE. This is the same time that Buddhism and Jainism evolved to make up the three ancient religions. The classical "golden age of Hinduism" lasted from 200 BCE to 500 CE. The period from roughly 650 to 1100 CE forms the early Middle Ages, in which classical Puranic Hinduism is established.

Hinduism, like all religions, has a belief system. However, Hinduism is a moral-encompassing way of life. It has a continuing cycle of entanglement in passions and the resulting birth, life, death, and rebirth. All aspects of a Hindu life, namely acquiring wealth (*artha*), fulfillment of desires (*kama*), and attaining liberation (*moksha*), are part of dharma, which encapsulates the "right way of living" and eternal harmonious principles in their fulfillment. Hindu thought accepts four proper goals or aims of human life:

Dharma-righteousness and ethics.
Artha (livelihood and wealth)

Kama (sensuality and pleasure)
Moksha (liberation and freedom)

Hinduism as *Sanātana Dharma* (Orthodox Hinduism) is the "eternal law" or the "eternal way." Sanātana Dharma referred to the "eternal" duties religiously ordained in Hinduism, duties such as honesty, refraining from injuring living beings (ahiṃsā), purity, goodwill, mercy, patience, forbearance, self-restraint, generosity, and asceticism. It is ultimately "nonsectarian."

In the Vedas, the most ancient of the world's scriptures, Sanātana Dharma refers to "timeless, eternal set of truths," and this is how Hindus view the origins of their religion.

Forgiveness is central to the religion. It is considered one of the six cardinal virtues in Hindu Dharma.

The religious basis for forgiveness in Hindu Dharma is that a person who does not forgive carries a burden of memories of the wrong, negative feelings, anger, and unresolved emotions. These negative emotions affect them presently and in the future.

In Hindu Dharma, not only should one forgive others but one must also seek forgiveness if one has wronged someone else. Forgiveness is to be sought from the individual wronged—as well as society at large—by acts of charity, purification, fasting, rituals, and meditative introspection.

Forgiveness for the Hindu Dharma has a feminine and a masculine side, which are represented by a goddess and her husband. Feminine Lakshmi forgives even when the one who does wrong does not repent. Masculine Vishnu, on the other hand, forgives only when the wrongdoer repents. On the feminine side, the highest level of forgiveness is when there is repentance from the wrongdoer.

Hindu scholars argue against carte blanche forgiveness. Unforgiveness is considered with murder and rape. They also question whether complete forgiveness allows for disrespect and social disorder and encourages crime. They believe that forgiveness is not same as reconciliation. Forgiveness in Hindu Dharma does not necessarily require that one reconcile with the offender or rule out reconciliation in some situations. Instead, forgiveness in Hindu philosophy is being compassionate, tender, and kind and letting go of the harm or hurt caused by someone or something else.

Forgiveness is essential for freeing oneself from negative thoughts and being able to focus on blissfully living a moral and ethical life (a dharmic life). In the highest self-realized state, forgiveness becomes the essence of one's personality; the persecuted person remains unaffected, without agitation, without feeling like a victim, and free from anger.

JAINISM

Jainism, traditionally known as Jain Dharma, is an ancient Indian religion. The origins are somewhat obscure, but most scholars date it to the ninth to seventh century BCE. However, Jainism believes that its religion is eternal and dates back to the first millennium.

Jainism is a transtheistic religion, holding that the universe was not created, and will exist forever. It is believed to be independent, having no creator, governor, judge, or destroyer. In this, it is unlike the Abrahamic religions, but it is similar to Buddhism.

Jains take five main vows: nonviolence, truth, not stealing, sexual continence, and non-possessiveness. Jains believe in helping one another. They also believe the universe is made up of six eternal substances: sentient beings or souls, non-sentient substance or matter, principle of motion, and the principle of rest, space, and time.

The religion has between four and twenty million followers, known as Jains, who reside mostly in India. Outside of India, some of the largest communities are in Canada, Europe, and the United States. Japan has a fast-growing community of converts.

In Jainism, forgiveness is one of the main virtues that needs to be cultivated. Jains ask for forgiveness from all creatures they may harm. This is in their prayers as well. Although vegetarian, they ask for forgiveness for harm to the living food they are eating. By practicing repentance, a soul gets rid of sins and commits no transgressions. Any transgressions that are committed must be forgiven.

BUDDHISM

Buddhism is a northern Indian religion or philosophical tradition based on a series of original teachings attributed to Gautama Buddha. Buddha means "Awakened One." Unlike Hinduism and Jainism, Buddhist arose from a spiritual leader.

Its origins date between the sixth and fourth centuries BCE. Buddhism arose in and around the ancient kingdom of Magadha, in the northeastern area of India and Nepal. It spread throughout Central, East, and Southeastern Asia. At one time or another, it influenced most of Asia.

It is the world's fourth-largest religion with more than 520 million followers (more than 7 percent of the global population). Buddhism encompasses a variety of traditions, beliefs, and spiritual practices.

The goal of Buddhism is to overcome suffering caused by desire and ignorance of reality's true nature, including impermanence and the nonexistence of the self. Most Buddhist traditions emphasize transcending the individual self through the attainment of Nirvana or by following the path of Buddhahood, ending the cycle of death and birth. They seek to follow a path toward virtuous perfection.

Buddha also taught the Four Noble Truths: the noble truth of suffering, the noble truth of the origin of suffering, the noble truth of the cessation of suffering, and the noble truth of the way to the cessation of suffering. The way to the cessation of suffering can be found in the Noble Eightfold Paths.

The Fourth Noble truth charts the method for attaining the end of suffering, known to Buddhists as the Noble Eightfold Path. The steps of the Noble Eightfold Path are right understanding, right thought, right speech, right action, right livelihood, right effort, right mindfulness, and right concentration.

Similarly to the Baha'i faith, Buddhism is more proactive. Forgiveness in Buddhism is seen as a practice to prevent harmful thoughts from causing problems in one's mental well-being. It recognizes that feelings of hatred have a lasting effect on the mind's karma. Buddhism encourages the cultivation of wholesome thoughts.

The Buddha taught about "karmic conditioning," which is a process in which a person's nature is shaped by their moral actions. Every action we take molds our character for the future. Both positive and negative traits can become magnified over time as we fall into habits. All of these cause us to acquire karma.

FORGIVENESS IN THE ABRAHAMIC RELIGIONS: JUDAISM, CHRISTIANITY, AND ISLAM

Abraham, the first of the Hebrew patriarchs, is considered the father of three great monotheistic religions: Judaism, Christianity, and Islam. The existence of Abraham is seen in texts from Mesopotamia dating 1996 BCE to 1821 BCE, in southern Iraq. His fame results from writings that recorded Abraham following everything asked of him by God. Included in God's direction, Abraham was to leave his home for a promised land where he and his descendants would create a great nation. The most significant demand God makes on Abraham is that he and his descendants totally commit to a belief in one and only one God. This is the foundation of Judaism, Christianity, and Islam.

Abraham conceived of two boys, each demanded by God. The first was with Hagar (the maid of Abraham's wife) because Sarah was not fertile. Hagar gave birth to Ishmael. God then told Abraham that Sarah could conceive and give birth to Isaac. Jews and Christians believe Isaac is the chosen leader, and Muslims believe both Ishmael and Isaac are chosen.

JUDAISM

The origins of Judaism date back to Abraham who was considered the first Jew. However, around the sixth or fifth century BCE, the Israelite religion became distinct. The Torah (the first five books of the Hebrew Bible: Genesis, Exodus, Leviticus, Numbers, and Deuteronomy) provide some of the historical documentation of Judaism.

In Judaism, if a person causes harm, but then sincerely and honestly apologizes to the wronged individual and tries to rectify the wrong, the wronged individual is encouraged, but not required, to grant forgiveness, which is written in the Mishneh Torah. The precedes the Bible, and the Torah is the first part of the Jewish Bible. It is the central and most important document of Judaism and has been used by Jews through the ages. Torah refers to the five books of Moses, which are known in Hebrew as Chameesha Choomshey Torah.

In Judaism, one must go "to those he has harmed" to be entitled to forgiveness. One who sincerely apologizes three times for a wrong committed against another has fulfilled their obligation to seek forgiveness. Murder is not forgiven by God, and may not be forgiven by the victim's family.

CHRISTIANITY AND FORGIVENESS

Christianity began in the first century CE, after Jesus died, and was said to be resurrected in 32 CE. It started as a small group of Jewish people in and around Jerusalem, and it spread quickly throughout the Roman Empire. Despite early persecution of Christians, it later became the state religion. It forms the basis of the New Testament in the Bible.

Christian beliefs consist of three parts: the Father (God himself), the Son (Jesus Christ), and the Holy Spirit. The essence of Christianity revolves around the life, death, and resurrection of

Jesus. Christians believe God sent his Son, Jesus, the Messiah, to save the world.

Among the religiously affiliated, Christians have the highest numbers worldwide at more than 2.54 billion in 2021, followed by Muslims (more than 1.92 billion), and Hindus (more than 1.07 billion).

Forgiveness is central to all forms of Christianity. It is a frequent topic in sermons and theological works because Christianity is about Jesus Christ. Christ first reveals forgiveness in the New Testament. Forgiveness is about redemption, and redemption is about forgiveness of sin.

Fundamental to Christian forgiveness is God will acknowledge forgiveness of man's sins when man asked for God's forgiveness of his sins. Unlike Judaism, God can forgive sins committed by people against people—since he can forgive every sin except for the eternal sin—and forgiveness from one's victim is not necessary for salvation. The most unforgiveable sin is blasphemy against God.

A really strange twist in the Christian religion is forgiving others begets being forgiven by God. How is it that when one forgives the wrongdoer, and the wronged forgives the wrongdoer, God forgives the wronged? If the wronged does not forgive the wrongdoer, then God cannot forgive the wronged. For what purpose? God is to forgive all sins, but consider Mark 11:25 and Matthew 6:14–15:

> And when you stand praying, if you hold anything against anyone, forgive them, so that your Father in heaven may forgive you your sins.") and Matthew 6:14-15, that follows the Lord's Prayer,

> "For if you forgive men when they sin against you, your heavenly Father will also forgive you. But if you do not forgive men their sins, your Father will not forgive your sins.

GRIEF, FORGIVENESS, ACCEPTANCE, AND REJECTION

Forgiveness is central to being a Christian, and forgiveness is not optional. It is a manifestation of submission to Christ and Christian believers. Jesus preaches forgiveness and mercy. This is based on the belief that God forgives sins through faith in the atoning sacrifice of Jesus Christ in his death.

The three exceptionally noted teachings of forgiveness by Jesus are the prodigal son, the Sermon on the Mount, and the Crucifixion. The Parable of the Prodigal Son is perhaps the best-known parable about forgiveness and refers to God's forgiveness for those who repent:

> The Prodical Son: (The Parable of the Lost Son) Luke 15;11-32. By the New International Version (NIV)
>
> 11 Jesus continued: "There was a man who had two sons. 12 The younger one said to his father, "Father, give me my share of the estate.' So he divided his property between them.
> 13 "Not long after that, the younger son got together all he had, set off for a distant country and there squandered his wealth in wild living. 14 After he had spent everything, there was a severe famine in that whole country, and he began to be in need. 15 So he went and hired himself out to a citizen of that country, who sent him to his fields to feed pigs. He longed to fill his stomach with the pods that the pigs were eating, but no one gave him anything.
> 17 "When he came to his senses, he said, "How many of my father's hired servants have food to spare, and here I am starving to death! 18 I will set out and go back to my father and say to him: Father, I have sinned against heaven and against you. 19 I am no longer worthy to be called your son; make me

like one of your hired servants." 20 So he got up and went to his father.

But while he was still a long way off, his father saw him and was filled with compassion for him; he ran to his son, threw his arms around him and kissed him.

21 "The son said to him, "Father, I have sinned against heaven and against you. I am no longer worthy to be called your son."

22 "But the father said to his servants, "Quick! Bring the best robe and put it on him. Put a ring on his finger and sandals on his feet. 23 Bring the fattened calf and kill it. Let's have a feast and celebrate. 24 For this son of mine was dead and is alive again; he was lost and is found." So they began to celebrate.

25 "Meanwhile, the older son was in the field. When he came near the house, he heard music and dancing. 26 So he called one of the servants and asked him what was going on. 27 Your brother has come," he replied, "and your father has killed the fattened calf because he has him back safe and sound."

The older brother became angry and refused to go in. So his father went out and pleaded with him. 29 But he answered his father, "Look! All these years I've been slaving for you and never disobeyed your orders. Yet you never gave me even a young goat so I could celebrate with my friends. 30 But when this son of yours who has squandered your property with prostitutes comes home, you kill the fattened calf for him!"

31 "'My son,' the father said, 'you are always with me, and everything I have is yours. 32 But we had to celebrate and be glad, because this brother of

yours was dead and is alive again; he was lost and is found." (Luke 15:11–32 NIV)

The Sermon on the Mount: Jesus repeatedly spoke of forgiveness in the Sermon on the Mount: "Blessed are the merciful, for they will be shown mercy" (Matthew 5:7 NIV).

> The Crucifixion: Luke 23 Then the whole assembly rose and led him off to Pilate. 2 And they began to accuse him, saying, "We have found this man subverting our nation. He opposes payment of taxes to Caesar and claims to be Messiah, a king." 3 So Pilate asked Jesus, "Are you the king of the Jews?" "You have said so," Jesus replied. As Jesus was about to be crucified on the cross, Jesus said, "Father, forgive them, for they know not what they do." (Luke 23:34 NIV)

These are all good example of forgiveness, but the art of forgiveness also becomes extreme in the Bible:

> . Mark 11:25 (NIV). "But I tell you who hear me: Love your enemies, do good to those who hate you, bless those who curse you, pray for those who mistreat you. If someone strikes you on one cheek, turn to him the other also."(

ISLAM

Islam is the act of submitting to the will of God, and a Muslim is a person who participates in the act of submission. To be correctly used, Islam or Islamic should describe the religion and its subsequent cultural concepts, and Muslim should only describe the followers of the religion of Islam. Muslims are monotheistic and worship one all-knowing God: Allah in Arabic. Followers of Islam aim to live a life of complete submission to Allah. They believe that nothing can happen without Allah's permission, but humans have free will.

Muslims have six main beliefs. They believe in Allah as the one and only God, *angeis*, holy books, predestination, Day of Judgment, and the belief in the prophets: Adam, Ibrahim (Abraham), Musa (Moses), Dawud (David), and Isa (Jesus).

The monotheistic religions of Abraham—Judaism, Christianity, and Islam—have different beliefs. Islam teaches that Jesus was one of the most important prophets of God, but he was not the Son of God, not divine, and not part of the Trinity. Muslims believe the creation of Jesus was similar to the creation of Adam (Adem), Abraham, and others. Christians believe Jesus was the incarnated Son of God, divine, and sinless. Judaism does not teach anything about Jesus.

Islam originated in Mecca and Medina at the start of the seventh century CE. In 610 CE, the Islamic prophet Muhammad began receiving what Muslims consider to be divine revelations, calling for submission to the one God, the expectation of the imminent Last Judgment, and caring for the poor and needy.

Islam went from a few ancient tribes to a huge empire. The caliphate is the name of the Muslim government that ruled the Islamic Empire during the Middle Ages. For a long time, the caliphate controlled Western Asia, North Africa, and parts of Europe.

More recent history of Islam concerns the political, social, economic, and cultural developments of Islamic civilization. It covers major historical centers of power and culture, including Arabia, Mesopotamia (modern Iraq), Persia (modern Iran), Levant (modern Syria, Lebanon, Jordan and Israel/Palestine), Egypt, Maghreb (northwest Africa), Al-Andalus (Iberia), Transoxiana (Central Asia), Hindustan (including modern Pakistan), North India and Bangladesh, and Anatolia (modern Turkey).

Islam teaches that Allah (God) is all-forgiving and is the original source of all forgiveness. Seeking forgiveness from Allah with repentance is a virtue. Allah forgives what is a virtue.

Numerous verses in the Quran and the Hadiths recommend

forgiveness. Islam also allows revenge to the extent harm done, but forgiveness is encouraged. Muhammad stated that forgiveness is derived from three wisdoms:

The most important wisdom of forgiveness is that it is merciful when the victim or guardian of the victim accepts money instead of revenge.

Forgiveness increases honor and prestige of the one who forgives. Forgiveness is not a sign of weakness, humiliation, or dishonor.

Forgiveness is honor, raises the merit of the forgiver in the eyes of Allah, and enables a forgiver to enter paradise.

Forgiveness makes reparation of the sins they may have committed at other occasions in life. It is considered God-forgiving people.

BAHÁ'Í FAITH

The Baha'i faith originated in Iran in 1863. The central figure of the religion is Baha'u'llah, and Baha'is consider him to be the latest in a series of divine messengers. Its beliefs are based on the manifestations of God, which are the multiple messengers sent by God to help humankind evolve and advance. Central to their beliefs is the unity of God, the unity of religion, and the unity of humanity.

Baha'is see themselves as a people with a mission to bring harmony and unity to the world, and this is reflected in their spiritual practices. The main purpose of life for Baha'is is to know and love God. Prayer, fasting, and meditation are the main ways of achieving this and making spiritual progress.

The countries with the largest Baha'i populations are India, the United States, Kenya, Vietnam, Congo, the Philippines, Zambia, South Africa, Iran, and Bolivia, ranging upward from 232,000 to just more than two million in India.

In terms of forgiveness, Abdu'l-Bahá (a Baha'i leader) wrote the *Promulgation of Universal Peace*:

> Humanity is not perfect. There are imperfections in every human being, and you will always become unhappy if you look toward the people themselves. But if you look toward God, you will love them and be kind to them, for the world of God is the world of perfection and complete mercy. Therefore, do not look at the shortcomings of anybody: see with the sight of forgiveness.

TYPES OF FORGIVENESS IN PSYCHOLOGY

Forgiveness is complex and not easy to resolve. To understand forgiveness, it is easier to discuss unforgiveness. The emotions associated with unforgiveness are bitterness, hostility, anger, and fear. These negative feelings and emotions are harmful to one's own health.

Unforgiveness is less situational and more dependent on how the wronged responds. If the underlying mental outlook is negative in the person wronged, a grudge may last—no matter the hurtful situation. Although a grudge can occur in anyone, underlying mental health is more dependent on the outcome than the situation. There is a double-edged sword in that unforgiveness can lead to anxiety and depression—and anxiety and depression can lead to unforgiveness.

Forgiveness is more situational, and there are five types:

> submissive
> exonerative
> forbearing
> threatening
> releasing

Exoneration and forbearance are closely related to relationships with family, relatives, friends, work associates, and colleague, and social situations.

SUBMISSIVE FORGIVENESS

In this type of forgiveness, the wronged forgives the wrongdoer no matter how severe or heinous the harm or crime. The wronged forgives the wrongdoer in the name of God. In other words, God exonerates all, and the wronged feels OK with God's forgiveness.

Psychologists state that forgiveness is not being submissive, passive, or compliant. It is a betrayal of trust and compassion when the other person repeats the offense. The offender must understand consequences and accountability. Although consequence and accountability are mentally healthy, the Bible and Christianity allow for submissive, passive, and compliant forgiveness.

There can be a philosophical tone to forgiveness. If someone hurts you, you can say, "I forgive you, but I cannot forgive what you have done to yourself!"

EXONERATIVE FORGIVENESS

Exoneration is complete forgiveness. Hard feelings, grudges, dislikes, and fear are totally gone. This releases any feeling of anger of resentment.

Several situations fall under exoneration. One situation is when the hurtful situation was a complete accident for which no fault or blame can be applied. This could also be considered an apology. This may be a situation where someone trips another person in a crowd, causing a fall. The person who fell forgives the person who caused the accident, and the person who caused the fall is also sorry.

A second situation that applies to exoneration is when the person who committed the offense is a child or is not capable of understanding the implications of their actions. In this situation, a child may take crayons and write on the wall in their bedroom.

The third situation occurs when the person who hurt you is truly sorry, takes full responsibility—without excuses—for what they did, asks for forgiveness, and gives you confidence that they will not knowingly repeat their bad action in the future.

The final event is reconciliation.

FORBEARING FORGIVENESS

Forbearance is when an offender either makes a partial apology or lessens their apology by suggesting that the person who is hurt is also partially to blame for their wrongdoing. The wrongdoer's forgiveness is not authentic, but the wronged should forgive but not forget. In this type, there is truly a feeling of legitimacy, authenticity, and respect. It is a warm feeling that does not require vigilance.

In some cases, after a sufficient period of good behavior, forbearance can rise to exoneration and full forgiveness.

THREATENING FORGIVENESS

This type of forgiveness is conditional or absent. The wronged may say, "I'll forgive you if you stop hurting me." The forgiveness from the wrongdoer or wronged is preceded by "if."

The wrongdoer does not even acknowledge that they have done anything wrong or gives an insincere apology, making no reparations. The wrongdoer will provide the wronged with an apology or ask for forgiveness. These wrongdoers usually have a mental health disorder, such as narcissism or sociopathology, were subjected to child abuse, are powerful, or have been betrayed.

RELEASING FORGIVENESS

Releasing does not exonerate the wrongdoer or require forbearance. There is no further need for a relationship. However, it does require the wronged to release the hurt. The preoccupation, rumination, and anger require mental release from all the negative thoughts so that mental health is restored. One is now free of the heavy burden of hurt, pain, betrayal, and anger. The essence of forgiveness is releasing the anger. Dwelling on the hurt allows the wrongdoer to be attached to the mind, which is not healthy. Maintaining the hurt is harmful. They should move forward with counselling or psychotherapy or talk to someone who can be trusted.

BIBLE VERSES

Forgiveness originates in the Bible, and it does so with numerous scriptures. The number of times that forgiveness appears in the Bible depends on the version of the Bible. In the King James Version, "forgiveness," or some form of the word, is used ninety-five times. The first-century rabbis taught that one ought to forgive three times. The number was based on the first and second chapters of Amos, an Old Testament prophet.

> BIBLE VERSES ASSOCIATED WITH PSYCHOLOGICAL TYPES SUBMISSIVE VERSES (All verses from the New International Version of the Bible)
>
> Romans 4:5. But people are counted as righteous, not because of their work, but because of their faith in God who forgives sinners. (Romans 4:5)

Repent, then, and turn to God, so that your sins may be wiped out, that times of refreshing may come from the Lord. (Acts 3:19)

But I say to you who hear: love your enemies, do good to those who hate you. (Luke 6:27)

Repay no one evil for evil, but give thought to do what is honorable in the sight of all. (Romans 12:17)

He is the propitiation for our sins, and not for ours only but also for the sins of the whole world. (1 John 2:2)

The times of ignorance God overlooked, but now he commands all people everywhere to repent. (Acts 17:30)

I am he who blots out your transgressions for my own sake, and I will not remember your sins. (Isaiah 43:25)

Let the wicked forsake his way, and the unrighteous man his thoughts; let him return to the Lord, that he may have compassion on him, and to our God. (Isaiah 55:7)

The Lord our God is merciful and forgiving, even though we have rebelled against him. (Daniel 9:9)

EXONERATIVE VERSES

Do not judge, and you will not be judged. Do not condemn, and you will not be condemned. Forgive, and you will be forgiven. (Luke 6:37)

A soft answer turns away wrath, but a harsh word stirs up anger. (Proverbs 15:1)

Blessed are the merciful, for they shall receive mercy. (Matthew 5:7)

Love prospers when a fault is forgiven, but dwelling on it separates close friends. (Proverbs 17:9)

Therefore, confess your sins to one another and pray for one another, that you may be healed. The prayer of a righteous person has great power as it is. (James 5:16)

I am writing to you, little children, because your sins are forgiven for his name's sake. (1 John 2:12)

FORBEARING AND THREATENING FORGIVENESS VERSES

But if you do not forgive others their sins, your father will not forgive your sins. (Matthew 6:15)

Hatred stirs old quarrels, but love overlooks insults. (Proverbs 10:12)

If my people who are called by my name humble themselves, and pray and seek my face and turn from their wicked ways, then I will hear from heaven and will forgive their sin and heal their land. (2 Chronicles 7:14)

So if you are offering your gift at the altar and there remember that your brother has something against you, leave your gift there before the altar and go.

> First be reconciled to your brother, and then come and offer your gift. (Matthew 5:23–24)

> And when you stand praying, if you hold anything against anyone, forgive them, so that your father in heaven may forgive you your sins. (Mark 11:25)

> I tell you, her sins—and they are many—have been forgiven, so she has shown me much love. But a person who is forgiven little shows only little love. (Luke 7:47)

> For I will be merciful toward their iniquities, and I will remember their sins no more. (Hebrews 8:12)

RELEASING VERSES

> And so I tell you, every kind of sin and slander can be forgiven, but blasphemy against the spirit will not be forgiven. (Matthew 12:31)

ONE UNFORGIVEABLE SITUATION IN CHRISTIANITY: BLASPHEMY

One eternal or unforgivable sin—blasphemy against the Holy Spirit—also known as the sin unto death, is specified in several passages of the Synoptic Gospels, including Mark 3:28–29, Matthew 12:31–32, Luke 12:10, Hebrews 6:4–6, Hebrews 10:26–31, and 1 John 5:16.

Blasphemy, as defined mostly in Christian and Islam religions or religion-based laws, is an insult that shows contempt, disrespect, or a lack of reverence concerning a deity, a sacred object, or something considered religiously inviolable. In religion and ethics, the inviolability of life, or the sanctity of life, is a principle of implied protection regarding aspects of sentient life that are said to be holy, sacred, or otherwise of such value that they are not to be violated.

A blasphemy law is a law prohibiting blasphemy, and blasphemy is the act of insulting or showing contempt or lack of reverence to a deity. Blasphemy laws argue that there is an established religion within a state or country. It also argues that blasphemy laws allows minority religions to exist within a state or country.

Anti-blasphemy laws oppose blasphemy laws. It is argued that the blasphemy laws prevent freedom of speech. Anti-blasphemy laws have only been passed between 2000 and 2020. Anti-blasphemy laws existed in thirty-two countries, but eighty-seven nations had hate speech laws that covered defamation of religion and public expression of hate against religious groups.

THE NEUROBIOLOGY OF FORGIVENESS

Personal offenses and harmful hurts can cause emotional pain, anger, betrayal, revenge, and retaliation in the victims who have been wronged. It is important to understand adaptation to the harmful event. It is important for social integration and mental health. Cognitive understanding is important in this adaptive mechanism. Forgiveness is a cognitive and emotional process that eradicates chronic hostility, rumination, and adverse effects.

Understanding the biological mechanisms in the brain for harm and hurtful situations, along with both forgiveness and unforgiveness, is important for understanding adaptation for social integration, survival, personal mental, and physical health.

There is a spectrum of hurtful situations, as well as various complex responses. We have divided hurtful events into three types: mild formidable hurt, moderate intensity hurt, and extreme hurt.

Examples of mild formidable hurt are having the boss at work degrade a person's work, especially in front of coworkers, or a friend verbally hurting another friend. Disrespect and rudeness fall into this category.

Examples of a moderate intensity hurt is being cheated on by a partner and an employee steeling from an employer.

Examples of extreme hurt are having a loved one murdered or spousal abuse.

In terms of forgiveness to these different degrees of hurt, there will be different responses in different parts of the brain. The different hurtful situations create difficulty in measuring activity in different parts of the brain. Much of the scientific studies to determine different parts of the brain activated by hurtful situations versus forgiveness has been studied by functional MRIs (fMRI).

Functional MRIs of the brain can determine the areas of activation to a response. How do these MRI determine brain activation? Functional magnetic resonance imaging measures brain activity by detecting changes associated with blood flow in the form of blood-oxygen levels. This technique relies on the fact that brain blood flow and neuronal (nerve) activation are coupled. When an area of the brain is in use, blood flow to that region increases. Special MRI units along with computers provide high-resolution images. The imaging is all dependent on using an MRI with high magnification and sophisticated technology.

Most all of the best studies on brain function and activation use functional MRIs. We provide a few studies for an understanding of how the brain functions in forgiveness and unforgiveness.

A study published by PMC (https://www.ncbi.nlm.nih.gov/pmc/articles/PMC3914861/) used functional MRI to study areas of activation in the brain for forgiveness and unforgiveness.

The neuroscientists found the following areas of the brain that were activated during forgiveness. These area include left middle temporal gyrus (LMTG), the left angular gyrus (LAG) and the inferior frontal gyrus (IFG), left ventromedial prefrontal cortex (LVPC), posterior cingulate gyrus (PCG), and right temporal parietal junction (rTPJ).

What does all of this mean in terms of response and behavior? We interpreted these areas of activation, which may be interpreted by neuroscientists. There is visual, language, and sensory integration

(LMTG). Social cognitive functions are involved (LAG). The area of the emotion and emotion regulation in conjunction with memory is involved (LVPC). Depending on cognitive emotions, there may be deactivation of an emotion (PCG). There is orientation to new stimuli (rTPJ).

The results of unforgiveness showed areas of activation that includes IFG (inferior frontal gyrus), MTG (middle temporal gyrus), AG (angular gyrus), and R (right hemisphere) and L (left hemisphere). Without going into specifics, the areas of the brain that are not activated are the areas that involve empathy and positive emotions.

In a study by Li and Lu (2017, they assessed 178 young adults (fifty-five men) who completed the tendency to forgive TTF scale and underwent a resting-state fMRI scan. There was lower brain activity in the right dorsomedial prefrontal cortex for those participants who had a lower tendency to forgive. The dorsomedial prefrontal cortex is associated with social perspective-taking abilities, as is the dorsolateral prefrontal cortex.[1]

In contrast, Fourie, Hortensius, and Decety (2020), in their review of the literature, hypothesize that the lateral prefrontal cortex, temporoparietal junction, and ventromedial prefrontal cortex are associated with a forgiveness response when unjustly hurt by others. In contrast to Lu and Li, these authors do not conclude whether brain structure or brain activity leads to the psychological response of the forgiver.[2]

Variation in results from study to study is often associated with scientific study design. The best result in a study occurs with controlling as many variables as possible. For example, if using volunteers, they should have psychological evaluation to prevent

---

[1] Li H., Lu J. (2017). "The neural association between tendency to forgive and spontaneous brain activity in healthy young adults." *Frontiers in Human Neuroscience,* 11, 561.DOI: 10.3389/fnhum.2017.00561. https://pubmed.ncbi.nlm.nih.gov/29209186/.

[2] Fourie, M. M., Hortensius, R. & Decety, J. (2020). "Parsing the components of forgiveness: Psychological and neural mechanisms." *Neuroscience & Biobehavioral Reviews,* 112, 437–451 https://doi.org/10.1016/j.neubiorev.2020.02.020.

oversensitive persons or narcissistic volunteers in the study, which will cause different results from a normal, healthy volunteer. The degree of wrongdoing will affect the results.

We provided three types of harmful conditions: mild formidable hurt, medium-intensity harm, and extreme harm. The best example of mild formidable harm is when an employee is admonished or criticized by the boss in front of other employees.

A study published by Italian psychologists and neuroscientists in *Front Hum Neuroscience* (2013) used functional MRIs to map the brain in forgiveness and similar scenarios.[3] This is a very controlled study using within subject controls where the normal volunteer is at rest with no activity (within subject control), and then the volunteer is given different hurtful scenarios by the person's boss in which the functional MRI maps activity in the brain as a response to the hurtful situation. Asking the volunteer to imagine situations is also used. They were asked to imagine hurtful situations when specifically prompted by imagining a hurtful scenario as compared to a neutral condition, which provided specific areas of activation in the brain

Imaging the brain in hurtful imagination stimulus was found in the following areas of the brain:

Right dorsal-medial prefrontal areas. This area of the brain is associated with the ability to reason about other people's mental states and form impressions of their character.

Left temporoparietal junction. This part of the brain is involved in the processing of information in terms of the ability of an individual to orient attention to new stimuli.

Medial temporal gyrus (MTG). This area of the brain serves language and semantic (returning to meaning of language or logic) memory processing,

---

[3] How the brain heals emotional wounds: the functional neuroanatomy of forgiveness (nih.gov).

Precuneus. This part of the brain is involved in a variety of complex functions, which include recollection and memory, integration of information (gestalt) relating to perception of the environment, cue reactivity, mental imagery strategies, episodic memory retrieval, and affective responses to pain.

The functional MRIs show specific areas of the brain that become activated when the person is asked to imagine a hurtful situation. The interpretation is incorporated into the brain for processing. There is processing of the language used for imagination. The brain interprets meaning and logic along with memory processing.

The new stimuli regarding other people's mental states form impressions of their character. There is then integration of information (gestalt) relating to perception of the presented imaginary hurt.

Evaluating emotional responsiveness as compared to preparatory neutral and hurtful scenarios, it was found a higher activation in anterior cingulate complex (ACC) and posterior cingulate cortex (PCC). ACC is involved in emotion assessment, emotion-related learning, and autonomic regulation. Within ACC, posterior ACC is implicated in emotional regulation, autonomic integration, and affect related to pain. ACC is implicated in autonomic control, visceral integration, and conditioned learning. Also it is implicated in several complex cognitive functions, such as empathy, impulse control, emotion, and decision-making.

The parahippocampal/occipital is part of the limbic system. The region plays an important role in memory encoding and retrieval. It is also associated with the visual part of the brain.

The right precuneus is involved in memory tasks, such as when people look at images and try to respond based on what they have remembered in regard to verbal questions about their spatial details. It is involved with the left prefrontal cortex in the recall of episodic memories, including past episodes related to the self.

The right inferior parietal cortex is involved in the perception of emotions in facial stimuli and interpretation of sensory information.

The inferior parietal lobule is concerned with language, mathematical operations, and body image.

The dominant (left) middle frontal gyrus plays a key role in the development of literacy, and the nondominant (right) middle frontal gyrus is responsible for numeracy.

Research has shown that the nondominant (right) superior frontal gyrus is involved in impulse control and that its activation modulates inhibitory control and motor urgency.

The results of the study regarding emotional responsiveness to a hurtful situation is compared to normal brain activity before the hurtful situation. The areas of the brain that activated during this hurtful situation provide expected results. The hurtful situation causes an emotional response that is evaluated. The emotion recognized is pain. This can trigger the autonomic nervous system, which includes the fight-versus-flight response. The brain retrieves any similar situation from memory through visualization. There is complex association with verbal questions and memory of prior verbal information. Sensory functions, such as facial expression and language, are perceived. After going through the emotional responses, evaluations, and associations, the brain performs impulse control and inhibitory control and motor urgency. The anticipatory part most likely activates the visual areas of the brain.

When the person had anticipation (pre-hurtful stimuli) and hurtful situations, the emotional response to a hurtful situation shows the brain's functional areas with increased activity as follows:

Bilateral striate and extrastriate visual cortex. This area involves visual and visual associate areas.

Sensorimotor frontoparietal areas. This area is involved in execution of movements related to self-awareness and language decoding.

Supplementary motor area. This is responsible for planning of complex movements.

Anterior MTG (middle temporal gyrus). This area is responsible for language processes

Anterior medial prefrontal areas. This area mediates decision-making and relies on long-term memory.

Left temporoparietal. This area is involved in language cognition, processing, and comprehension of both written and spoken language.

Premotor areas. This area prepares the body's muscles for exact movements and specific muscle control.

Subgenual cingulate cortex. This area regulates emotion, and degeneration in this area correlates to depressed mood.

Thalami. The thalamus is a mostly gray matter structure of the diencephalon that has many essential roles in human physiology. The thalamus is composed of different nuclei that each serve a unique role, ranging from relaying sensory and motor signals, as well as regulation of consciousness and alertness.

Cerebellum. This has a role in coordination.

In this situation, there is no comparison between normal and hurtful situations, but there is anticipation of the hurt, which then becomes hurtful. The areas in the brain that become activated can explain the person's psychological response. As the hurt is directed to the person, there is language interpretation and execution of movements related to self-awareness. Between the anticipation and hurt, the brain plans and prepares for complex movements, possibly a physical or verbal fight. Long-term memories of prior hurtful situations are evaluated in the form of mediating or making a decision about how to manage the hurt of the person creating the hurt.

The brain enlists specific muscles in terms of their use. Emotions are involved. All of these signals pass through the thalamus, which processes sensory and motor signals. Motor signals are sent to the cerebellum for coordination. This anticipatory and hurtful situation creates activity in the brain similar to the fight-versus-flight response in the autonomic nervous system.

The final results of brain activation in forgiveness and unforgiveness supports the area of activation in forgiveness is associated with emotion and empathy. Whereas this area is eliminated in unforgiveness. The detailed results of this study are noted below.

FORGIVENESS RESULTS IN BRAIN ACTIVATION AREAS

Activation in the brain starts at OCC occipital cortex and branches to five other areas of the brain, starting with medial temporal gyrus (MTG), anterior cingulate cortex (ACC), posterior cingulate cortex (PCC), inferior parietal lobule (IPL), precuneus (PRE). Then it travels to dorsolateral prefrontal cortex (DLPFC) and posterior cingulate cortex, (PCC) and the PCC returns to the anterior cingulate cortex (ACC).

INTERPRETATION OF BRAIN AREA ACTIVATION IN FORGIVENESS

At the initiation of the process in the brain, the visual part of the brain is activated. There is cognitive language interpretation. The anterior cingulate complex is activated, which is involved in complex cognitive functions, such as empathy, impulse control, emotion, and decision-making and resolves conflict response. There is a cognitive emotional interaction. Additional processing occurs related to sensorimotor integration, spatial attention, and visuomotor and auditory processing.

The last integrative function is a collection and memory, integration of information (gestalt) relating to perception of the environment, cue reactivity, mental imagery strategies, episodic memory retrieval, and affective responses to pain. After this preliminary integration, the information returns to cognitive conflict management and memory association. There is deactivation of negative thoughts. The last step is the final forgiveness area of the brain involved in functions, such as empathy, impulse control, emotions, and decision-making.

INTERPRETATION OF BRAIN AREA ACTIVATION IN UNFORGIVENESS

At the initiation of the process in the brain, the visual part of the brain is activated. From the sight signal, activation begins with language interpretation and cognitive social interpretation. There is sensory integration. There is further activation that is involved in recollection and memory, integration of information (gestalt) relating to perception of the environment, cue reactivity, mental imagery strategies, episodic memory retrieval, and affective responses to pain. There is a cognitive emotional interaction. The area of complex empathy, impulse control, emotion, and decision-making is activated. The medial temporal gyrus that has already been activated branches to two other areas. The middle temporal gyrus is responsible for language interpretation and sensory interpretation along with cognitive function.

From the functional middle temporal gyrus, the next area of brain activation is involved with decision-making, working memory, conflict management, and mood regulation. At the same time, the area of brain activation is involved in recollection and memory and integration of information (gestalt) relating to perception of the environment.

After these areas of activation, the last area of the brain to be activated is unforgiveness. This is the area involved with sensorimotor integration, spatial attention, and visuomotor and auditory processing. This indicates that the person is not willing to forgive. It should be noted that the area of the brain that is not activated in unforgiveness is the area of emotional empathy.

THE PSYCHOLOGY OF FORGIVENESS

There are different definitions and discussion of forgiveness. Psychologists generally define forgiveness as a conscious, deliberate decision to release feelings of resentment or vengeance toward a person or group who has harmed you, regardless of whether they actually deserve your forgiveness. Forgiveness does not mean forgetting, condoning, or excusing offenses.

An excellent psychological definition of forgiveness is empathy, compassion, and understanding toward the person who hurt you. That element makes forgiveness both a virtue and a powerful construct in positive psychology.

There can be confusion over what forgiveness is and is not. Forgiveness is not excusing or explaining away the offender's responsibility or free will. Forgiveness does not minimize the hurt. Forgiveness is not acknowledging and showing negative emotions. Negative emotions are in the process of forgiveness, only to be recognized, but then the person must move into a positive, empathetic forgiveness. Forgiveness is not pardoning or reconciling for someone's wrongdoing. Forgiveness is accountability, which cannot be ignored.

Researchers agree that forgiveness is distinct from several other related constructs, such as pardoning (a legal term for absolving a person of his/her guilt), condoning (which entails that the offense is justifiable), excusing (which entails that there are mitigating factors that led to the offense), forgetting (which suggests that the offense is not consciously accessible), or reconciling (which involves the restoration of the relationship). Forgiveness also differs from defense mechanisms such as denial, suppression, repression, and dissociation because all of these involve a refusal to acknowledge the offense.

Psychologists have found that some people are naturally more forgiving than others. Psychological research has found that more forgiving types tend to have higher levels of agreeableness and lower levels of neuroticism. People who have a tendency to ruminate are generally less quick to forgive since they are more likely to hold onto grudges or hurt feelings.

Psychology has also found that people who have a religious faith seem to have a greater ability to forgive. As noted earlier, all the major religions value forgiveness.

Research has shown that forgiveness is linked to mental health outcomes, such as reduced anxiety, depression, and major psychiatric disorders, fewer physical health issues, and lower mortality rates.

EMOTIONAL FORGIVENESS AND DECISIONAL FORGIVENESS

There has been controversy in psychology regarding emotional forgiveness and decisional forgiveness:

Emotional forgiveness: Emotional forgiveness is the replacement of negative, unforgiving emotions with positive, other-oriented ones.

Decisional forgiveness: Decisional forgiveness is defined as the behavioral intention statement that one seeks to reduce one's negative behavior and (if possible and appropriate) restore positive behavior toward the offender.

In general, there are differences between the two. Emotional forgiveness differs substantially from the mere decision to forgive. The fact that only those in the emotional forgiveness condition forget offense-relevant traits is an indicator that complete forgiveness depends on emotional involvement.

Nevertheless, even when making a sincere decision to forgive, one may still feel emotionally unforgiving (e.g., angry, resentful, and hurt) toward the offender. Emotional forgiveness, in turn, is considered the replacement of negative emotions with positive ones (e.g., empathy, love, and compassion).

There is a high correlation between the psychological studies regarding emotional forgiveness and decisional forgiveness and the neurobiological brain activation mapping studies with functional MRIs. Areas of the brain that are involved with forgiveness, legitimately, are the emotional and empathetic areas of the brain. This correlates to psychological and emotional forgiveness. The brain, in emotional forgiveness, uses cognitive functions, which make decisions, but the dominant area in emotional forgiveness is the areas of the brain involved with emotions and empathy.

Decisional forgiveness is more like the unforgiveable part of the brain that is activated.

There is an excellent study[4] from the Department of Psychology at the University of Munich, Germany: "Forgive and Forget: Differences between Decisional and Emotional Forgiveness."

FORGIVENESS INTERVENTION

Forgiveness does not require intervention when it is immediate exoneration and, to a degree, forbearance. To forgive and forget is the ultimate goal, but in some cases, the forgiveness process is more complex and takes time.

Intervention is needed when a person continues with problems forgiving, which takes some time to process. It is difficult to break this down in terms of time, but it certainly is not immediate or within a day or two. Anger, hostility, betrayal, and rumination get in the way of forgiving. This may be the situation with mild formidable hurt and medium-intensity hurt. Total unforgiveness may occur in either one of these if no forgiveness occurs and there is a persistence of anger, hostility, or guilt.

We propose three types of intervention:

Self-help. This can most likely be helpful in mild formidable and medium-intensity hurt.

Psychological intervention with medium-intensity hurt.
Psychological and psychiatric help in extreme hurt.

---

[4] https://www.ncbi.nlm.nih.gov/pmc/articles/PMC4422736/

SELF-HELP

Forgiveness is a process that does not happen immediately in most situations. Depending on the severity of the hurt, it can take a long time—even years in some cases. The scientific community says it is a process with various steps.

Step 1: Acknowledge the hurt.
Step 2: Consider how the hurt and pain have affected you.
Step 3: Accept that you cannot change the past.
Step 4: Determine whether or not you will forgive.
Step 5: Repair the relationship with the person who hurt you.
Step 6: Learn what forgiveness means to you.
Step 7: Forgive the person who wronged you. In some cases, this will be silent.

With forgiveness or unforgiveness, the key is acknowledging the hurt. All these steps can possibly be achieved, even in unforgiveness. The main issues with unforgiveness are anger, hostility, and rumination, which can persist if not unchecked.

Acknowledgement requires one to evaluate the hurt, who initiated the hurt, and acknowledge the feelings associated with the hurt.

Consideration is an important step because one decides to forgive or not forgive. This also takes into account consequences. Forgiveness will allow a person to forgive and forget, which leads to good mental and physical health, and unforgiveness will cause anger and hostility.

One must accept the fact that the hurtful incident occurred and cannot be reversed. This is not total acceptance; it is understanding consideration.

In the understanding process, one makes choices and determines to forgive or not forgive. The forgiveness process will restore self-esteem and relationships. Unforgiveness will end the process and cause anger and hostility.

When everything calms down, and there is no more anger or hostility, the relationship can be repaired. Letting the wrongdoer know about your hurt and discussing the issue can lead to a repair of the relationship. In some cases, this can be done immediately, in a few days or weeks, or several years. One can decide not to forgive, but this will require self-healing by releasing the anger and hostility. The person must repair themselves to rebuild mental and physical health.

Life is filled with learning processes. Hurtful situations will occur often in life. Learning how to deal with the hurt will create strength and self-esteem. After each forgiveness process, one will learn how to manage the next one.

The path to total forgiveness has many twists and turns, but when it is accomplished and finalized, it releases a heavy burden.

Awareness of the wrongdoer's mental state is also important. It is impossible to forgive a person with a personality disorder, such as a narcissist or a psychopath. They have no empathy. Murderers are usually psychopaths.

ANGER MANAGEMENT

In mild formidable and medium-intensity hurt, anger may persist. One can approach anger with a self-help process.

There are different approaches to the intervention of anger. The main goal is to get rid of anger and hostility. One model is to use three main approaches: expressing, suppressing, and calming. Expressing your angry feelings in an assertive—but not aggressive—manner is the healthiest way to express anger. To do this, you have to learn how to make clear what your needs are—and how to get them met—without hurting others. Start by considering these twelve anger management thoughts:

Become calm.
Think before you speak.
Once you're calm, express your anger.

Get some exercise.
Take a timeout.
Identify possible solutions.
Stick with "I" statements.
Use humor to release tension.
Open communication.
Practice relaxation skills.
Don't hold a grudge.
Know when to seek help.

Before any progress can be made, deep breaths, isolating, or going for a walk to calm down provides time to think about how to manage the anger and discuss the issues with the person who is causing the pain and hurt, which creates anger in yourself. Consulting a trusted person to describe the incident and how to manage it can be helpful.

After becoming calm and thinking through everything, one can express their needs and concerns. This should be done with minimal emotion and no confrontation. Discussion should be clear and noncontrolling.

Physical activity, such as jogging or brisk walking, can help relieve stress. However, doing something like power weightlifting can cause more anger. The activity should be fun to relieve the stress. Listening to music or reading a book can also reduce stress.

Taking a break from stressful activities is helpful. This time can be used to meditate or pray.

All of the techniques noted above should provide solutions for the anger problem. A solution is to forgive and forget. Conflict resolution can be another solution.

Do not blame; instead, take ownership of the situation by saying "I." Example: "I am upset with the way you hurt my feelings."

Using humor can help eliminate anger. Finding something humorous in the hurtful situation can reduce or eliminate anger.

The key to reducing or eliminating anger is open communication between the wrongdoer and the wronged. When communication is completely shut down, no progress is made toward mending the hurt and preventing anger.

Relaxation techniques and mindfulness often work for lower-intensity anger like frustration, hurtful situations, or annoyance. Practice deep breathing exercises, imagine a relaxing scene, or repeat a calming word or phrase: "Others may hurt me, but I love myself." You might also listen to music, write in a journal, or do a few yoga poses—whatever it takes to encourage relaxation.

Holding a grudge is stressful and harmful to your health. It is mentally consuming. A good method for getting rid of anger is forgiveness. We have come full circle to the benefits of forgiveness.

Learning to control anger can be a challenge for everyone at times. Seek help if your anger seems out of control, causes you to do things you regret, or hurts those around you.

Religion can play an important role in dealing with anger and promoting forgiveness. All religions, as we previously pointed out, have forgiveness.

PSYCHOLOGICAL INTERVENTION WITH MEDIUM-INTENSITY HURT

Optimal outcomes or results are in the presence of a therapist or psychologist in both the Enright Forgiveness Model and Worthington's Five-Step REACH Model.

Enright's forgiveness therapy process model uses a twenty-step system to move people through four phases:

uncovering one's negative feelings (anger) about the offense
deciding to forgive
working toward forgiveness of the offending person
discovering and releasing emotions.

Enright has shown this model is effective in various one-one-one interventions, including a study that showed it alleviated depression, anxiety, and PTSD in women who had experienced spousal emotional abuse. This study is entitled "The effects of forgiveness therapy on depressed, anxious, and posttraumatic stress for women after spousal emotional abuse" (Journal of Consulting and Clinical Psychology, 2006).

This study and others show that these cognitive exercises can help people see the other person as a wounded human being instead of stereotyping them and defining them by their hurtful actions.

PRELIMINARY STEPS AND PHASES OF THE ENRIGHT FORGIVENESS MODEL

Who hurt you?
How deeply were you hurt?
On what specific incident will you focus?
What were the circumstances at the time?
Was it morning or afternoon?
Was it cloudy or sunny?
What was said? How did you respond?

PHASE 1: UNCOVERING YOUR ANGER

How have you avoided dealing with anger?
Have you faced your anger?
Are you afraid of exposing your shame or guilt?
Has your anger affected your health?
Have you been obsessed with the injury or the offender?
Do you compare your situation to that of the offender?
Has the injury caused a permanent change in your life?
Has the injury changed your worldview?

PHASE 2: DECIDING TO FORGIVE

Decide that what you have been doing hasn't worked. Be willing to begin the forgiveness process. Decide to forgive.

PHASE 3: WORKING ON FORGIVENESS

Work toward understanding.
Work toward compassion.
Accept the pain.
Give the offender a gift.

PHASE 4: DISCOVERY AND RELEASE FROM EMOTIONAL PRISON

Discover the meaning of suffering.
Discover your need for forgiveness.
Discover that you are not alone.
Discover the purpose of your life.
Discover the freedom of forgiveness.

I recommend Robert Enright's *Forgiveness Is a Choice*.

Worthington's REACH Forgiveness Model also aims to find compassion for the wrongdoer. The five-step process helps people address their hurt, find empathy for the person who hurt them, reach forgiveness, and hold onto that forgiveness over time.

Worthington's model has been applied more often in group settings. Despite the differences in the interventions, both models promote forgiveness and the mental health benefits that go along with it. In a meta-analysis of fifty-four forgiveness studies, Worthington found that both his and Enright's models helped people forgive and improved their mental health (Journal of Consulting and Clinical Psychology, 2014).

There is a strong dose-response relationship between the amount of time people spend practicing forgiveness and the amount of forgiveness they are successful at experiencing.

When a therapist has people for a six-hour group session, they can forgive and reduce their levels of depression and anxiety.

Forgiveness is an important feature in couple's therapy; betrayal and resentment frequently occur in relationships where one person is hurt by infidelity.

Worthington's five-step technique of forgiveness is called REACH:

REACH, stands for the following:

Recall the hurt.
Empathize with the one who hurt you.
Altruistic gift of forgiveness (offer).
Commitment to forgive (make).
Hold on to the forgiveness.

RECALLING THE HURT

The natural response to hurt are feelings of fear and/or anger. With fear, one wants to run away. Anger promotes a desire to attack. Mental and physical avoidance are not unusual. Mental avoidance consists of trying to forget or distract the mind from focusing on painful thoughts related to the event. Physical avoidance is easy. At this stage, forgiveness is out of the question. This is more of a survival process. However, with the recall process, staying calm and relaxed is helpful. While thinking of the hurtful situation, deep breathing techniques and relaxation techniques must be done.

EMPATHY FOR THE WRONGDOER

This opens communication. It queries why the wrongdoer did what he or she did. We try to find a plausible explanation as to why the wrongdoer did what they did. This process is to live and let go. Part of this process is thinking that people who attack others are usually in a state of fear, anger, or hurt.

THE ALTRUISTIC GIFT OF FORGIVENESS

Altruism is the selfless concern for the well-being of others. This is a situation where you hurt someone and they forgive you, which eliminates your guilt. It is like receiving a gift. Likewise, when you forgive the wrongdoer, you are giving them a gift. Giving gifts relieves stress and increases self-esteem.

A COMMITMENT TO FORGIVENESS

The commitment to forgive should be said verbally to the wrongdoer. This can be done in the presence of another person or a therapist. Another technique is a letter of forgiveness. A church group also will share empathy for the situation.

HOLD ON TO THE FORGIVENESS

Holding on to the forgiveness means the memory of the hurtful event will fade with the emotions. One must interrupt all thoughts related to revenge and self-pity.

Religion can play an important role in dealing with anger and promoting forgiveness. All religions, as we previously pointed out, have forgiveness.

PSYCHOLOGICAL AND PSYCHIATRIC INTERVENTION IN EXTREME HURT

In extreme hurt, the situations involved are so harmful to a victim's mental and physical health that they require psychiatric or psychological treatment. Examples of extreme hurt or harm include murder of a loved one, witnessing a mass murder or a traumatic death (e.g., a motor vehicle accident), spousal abuse, child abuse, and sexual abuse.

Extreme hurt results in severe persistent anger and hostility that affect mental and physical health. Fear and fight-or-flight responses can occur. The hurt can lead to depression, anxiety, and post-traumatic stress disorder. All of these mental health disorders are beyond self-help techniques.

Although Enright and Worthington's forgiveness models have helped in some of these mental health disorders, if they fail, more intensive techniques are in order. Psychoanalysis, cognitive therapy, medications, and other psychological and psychiatric techniques are needed to achieve forgiveness. The goal is to achieve mental and physical health and restore a positive life.

PHYSICAL HEALTH RESPONSES TO FORGIVENESS

Much has been said about forgiveness and mental health, but very little has been said about the effects of forgiveness and physical health.

The correlation between forgiveness and physical health has been documented with research. Studies have shown that individuals with forgiveness as a personality trait have overall better physical health. Individuals who choose to forgive another after a transgression have lower blood pressure. This is theorized to be due to lower levels of stress hormones.

Direct influences include reducing hostility, which is inversely correlated to physical health, and unforgiveness due to chronic stress reduces the immune system in the individual.

Indirect influences are more related to forgiveness as a personality trait, and forgiving people have more social support and less stress. Relational forgiveness is documented in less stressful marriages. Indirect evidence also finds ease of forgiveness is related to personality traits that are correlated with physical health.

Hostility is associated with unforgiveness. Studies have shown that hostility is associated with poor coronary performance. Forgiveness is the act of letting go of hostility. Heart patients who are treated with therapy that includes forgiveness to reduce hostility have improved cardiac health compared to those who are treated with medicine alone (McCullough, Michael, and Charlotte Vanoyen, "The Psychology of Forgiveness." *Handbook of Positive Psychology*, 2002).

Forgiveness may also lead to better physical health. This applies to both self-forgiveness and forgiveness to others.

SUMMARY

Forgiveness is as old as ancient times, and it is found in all religions. Forgiveness is a complex psychosocial emotion. This is reflected by the many areas of the brain that are involved in forgiveness. Forgiveness is an emotion-focused coping strategy that can reduce stressful situations. The goal of forgiveness is to eliminate anger, hostility, and resentment. We provided ways to do this, and we also provided mechanisms to adjust to situations where forgiveness may not come to fruition. The purpose of this chapter is to create awareness of all the psychosocial aspects of forgiveness.

CHAPTER 4
GRIEF ACCEPTANCE, PERSONAL ACCEPTANCE AND PERSEVERANCE

> Understanding is the first step to acceptance, and only with acceptance can there be recovery.
> — J. K. Rowling, *Harry Potter and the Goblet of Fire*

Acceptance is a term with several meanings. It can be used personally to accept a gift, a handshake, or a hug. It is used in business to accept a negotiated price. In law, it is used to accept a contract. One can accept an invitation or consider being accepted into a group.

Acceptance is also associated with accepting the self and accepting grief. Acceptance can be an act of believing or accepting. The definition overlaps with tolerance, but acceptance and tolerance are not synonyms. Similarly related is the acceptance of beliefs, ideas, and opinions. We call this social tolerance or social acceptance. Both acceptance of grief and social acceptance are incorporated in psychology.

According to Wikipedia, acceptance in human psychology is a person's assent to the reality of a situation and recognizing a process or condition—often a negative or uncomfortable situation—without attempting to change it or protest it. The concept is close in meaning to acquiescence, which is derived from the Latin *acquiesce* (to find rest in).

Acquiescence is to assent tacitly, submit or comply silently or without protest, agree, or consent.

GRIEF ACCEPTANCE

Acceptance in grief is the last stage of the grieving process. However, it should be noted that all stages of grieving may return at intervals. Acceptance does not necessarily mean the whole grieving process no longer exists.

Acceptance in grief means embracing the present—considered bad—in order to shape the future. It does not mean that we no longer can think about the horrific or terrible incident or the death of a loved one. Out of sight does not have to mean out of mind since the brain has a strong memory.

Grief acceptance is multifactorial, depending on the person's mental and physical health. Acceptance may mean there are no other choices. A person with terminal cancer has to accept the situation and do so rather quickly compared to a loved one overseeing the process of dying.

A person with a disability who has a caretaker die may take a long time to deal with the loss and may never accept the loss. On the other hand, a caregiver who has a disabled partner die may accept the situation more readily because they no longer have to deal with the partner's disability. They may feel freer now.

The mental state for acceptance is important. A person who is mentally healthy can go through the process of acceptance. This is relative, but a person who has core values, such as self-respect, respect for others, honesty, and compassion, is better able to go through the last stage of grief (acceptance). Persons with generalized anxiety disorder, PTSD, phobias, and depressive disorders will have more difficulties with acceptance. It can be achieved with treatment of the underlying mental issues. Those persons with personality disorders, such as narcissism, paranoia, delusional disorder, sociopathy, and psychopathy are incapable of grieving and cannot go through the last stage of acceptance.

There is a caveat to grief acceptance. When another person causes criminal harm to a person or a loved one, acceptance is not complete until the person causing the crime is brought to justice. If there is no justice, acceptance may last indefinitely.

Grief acceptance does not mean that the person feels good or right about a bad situation or personal loss. Many people dealing with grief acceptance never feel free of the loss or bad situation. A problem is accepting the new reality that cannot be changed and coping with the new reality and relationships.

Grief acceptance is not the same as denial. Denial is one of the five stages of grieving.

As with almost everything in life, grief acceptance depends on choices and responsibility. One can choose to stay stuck in grieving or accept the situation for what it is. Getting unstuck may require talking to a trusted friend or family member. It may require counseling for a period of time to reach a level where one is content and thinking less and less about the grief.

Acceptance can occur through mindfulness.

SELF-ACCEPTANCE

In simple terms, self-acceptance is a current satisfaction with self. It is the process of appreciation, validating, and supporting the self, despite negative or deficiencies from past experiences or behaviors. People have trouble accepting themselves because of grief, guilt, trauma, or a perceived lack of motivation.

Some people have the misconception that if people are happy with themselves, it means that they would not change anything about themselves. Changing things they do not like about themselves should create more self-acceptance, which is better than rejection of the self. Therefore, to accept yourself means to no longer reject yourself. Social rejection can lead to poor self-acceptance.

THE PSYCHOLOGY OF SELF-ACCEPTANCE

Self-acceptance is an individual's satisfaction or happiness with oneself, and it is thought to be necessary for good mental health.[5]

Self-acceptance involves the understanding of self. Understanding takes into account a realistic awareness involving strengths and weaknesses and knowing that the person is unique. Self-acceptance develops into feelings, which is self-esteem. Both of these are considered a human norm.

Self-esteem refers to how a person feels about themselves—whether one's feelings are generally good, worthwhile, and valuable. Self-acceptance is simply acknowledging and accepting oneself. Self-acceptance alludes to a far more global affirmation of self. When a person is self-accepting, they are able to embrace all facets of themselves—not just the positive feelings. Self-acceptance creates self-esteem.

Self-esteem should not be confused with self-efficacy. Self-efficacy is beliefs about performing up to personal standards, producing desired results, and making important life decisions. Self-efficacy is related to the personality traits of extroversion and subjective well-being.

Accepting oneself likely creates good choices, which creates opportunities and allows for improving the self. Self-acceptance means having the ability to achieve one's goals and develop other abilities, such as creativity. It is a self-enabling process.

How is ego differentiated from self-esteem and self-acceptance? Ego is defined as a person's sense of self-importance. Ego is a thinking process in which the person thinks they are important or extremely important. Self-esteem is feeling good about oneself and having confidence in oneself. Self-acceptance is having an awareness of ego and self-esteem. One can have poor self-esteem and a big ego. Self-acceptance creates a difficulty dealing with the two.

---

[5] Shepard, Lorrie A. (1978). "Self-Acceptance: The Evaluative Component of the Self-Concept Construct." *American Educational Research Journal.* 16 (2): 139–160. doi:10.2307/1162326. JSTOR 1162326.

QUALITY AND QUANTITY OF SELF-ACCEPTANCE

Having quality self-acceptance means having a positive perception and attitude of the self. Having quality self-acceptance means not being critical of the self or confused about one's identity. They do not wish they were any different. Some people have problems remembering a person's name or forgetting names. It would not be good to dislike oneself for the problem; instead, accept it and try to improve on the problem.

There cannot be too much self-acceptance. In fact, with mindfulness, one is aware of oneself and moment-to-moment awareness.

PSYCHOLOGICAL EVALUATION

People who feel isolated and lonely and excluded can develop anxiety and/or depression. Loneliness and isolation frequently occur with grief, whether it is the loss of a loved one or the loss of self-identity. One may think that punishing oneself enough will cause change, but this will only create more negativity. Accepting this negativity can provide a chance for change.

In addition, staying isolated and lonely can lead to physical health issues, such as not eating well, not sleeping, and infections and other ailments.

Self-acceptance in psychology is promoted as positive psychology therapy or the promotion of well-being. It reveres self-negativity.

Self-esteem comes from self-awareness. Knowing the things one does not like about oneself can lead to positive change. This creates a better opinion of the self and higher self-esteem.

Self-acceptance is the awareness of self. Awareness of the self is also present in mindfulness.

MINDFULNESS FOR SELF-ACCEPTANCE

MEANING of MINDFULNESS

Mindfulness is not meditation, but meditation can be a tool used in mindfulness.

The American Psychological Association (2012), defines mindfulness as "a moment-to-moment awareness of one's experience without judgment. In this sense, mindfulness is a state and not a trait. While it might be promoted by certain practices or activities, such as meditation, it is not equivalent to or synonymous with them."

Meditation is defined as a practice in which an individual uses a technique for focusing the mind on a particular object, thought, or activity—to train attention and awareness, and achieve a mentally clear and emotionally calm and stable state of mind. The Bible uses meditation as deep contemplation, a turning over and around in the mind to gain greater understanding and be changed by God's truth. Meditation is a tool of learning that can be abused. Yet, instead of avoiding it, we should use it with care, biblical understanding, and respect. Religious meditation is not mindfulness or mindfulness meditation.

A prayer is a solemn request for help or expression of thanks addressed to God or an object of worship. Prayer in the Hebrew Bible is an evolving means of interacting with God, most frequently through a spontaneous, individual, unorganized form of petitioning and/or thanking. Prayer is not meditation or mindfulness. Prayer is concerned with talking, conversing, and making requests be known. Meditation is concerned with a stillness, where one serves as a witness of one's own mind in order to listen and observe what is occurring within. Meditation is also a connection with God or Universal Spirit.

Mindfulness is not psychotherapy or counseling, but it is an individual-based activity. It is a sense of awareness, which can be practiced. Anyone can do it. One can think of it as a mind-heart-body process. Osteopathic medicine teaches this philosophical type of medicine.

Mindfulness is an awareness of the present without being judgmental. For example, sitting alone in a forest, seeing rays of light through the trees, and feeling calmness throughout one's body creates mindfulness. There is nothing to judge. One is only in the present. The mind can wonder to many thoughts, but staying in the present is important. If the mind moves to other thoughts, it is important to come back to the present and absorb the smell of the forest, the sight of the sun through the trees, the slow heartbeat, and the feeling of warmth in the body.

In grieving, one can be aware of the loss or negativity and bring the awareness to a positive reality that the loss is real, but it is time to move forward. When negative feelings of loss arise, this awareness can bring us back to the present reality. There is a conscious effort to face that which is occurring now.

Mindfulness is the quality or state of being conscious or aware of something. In addition, it is a mental state achieved by focusing one's awareness on the present moment—while calmly acknowledging and accepting one's feelings, thoughts, and bodily sensations. It can also be used as a therapeutic technique.

Merriam-Webster defines mindfulness as the practice of maintaining a nonjudgmental state of heightened or complete awareness of one's thoughts, emotions, or experiences on a moment-to-moment basis.

Wikipedia defines mindfulness as the psychological process of bringing one's attention to the internal and external experiences occurring in the present moment, which can be developed through the practice of meditation and other training.

The Greater Good Science Center at the University of California at Berkeley defines mindfulness in this way: "Mindfulness means maintaining a moment-by-moment awareness of our thoughts, feelings, bodily sensations, and surrounding environment."

The Mindful Awareness Research Center at the University of California at Los Angeles defines mindfulness in this way: "Mindful awareness is the moment-by-moment process of actively and openly observing one's physical, mental and emotional experiences."

The Mayo Clinic defines mindfulness in this way: "Mindfulness is the act of being intensely aware of what you're sensing and feeling every moment without interpretation or judgment."

HISTORY OF MINDFULNESS FROM EAST TO WEST

Mindfulness originated from the ancient Buddhist religion more than 2,500 years ago in India. The concept of mindfulness traces to the Pali word *ssati*, which in the Indian Buddhist tradition implies "moment-to-moment awareness of present events" and "remembering to be aware of something." It also implies *vipassana*, which means insight cultivated by meditation. Sati is one of the elements of enlightenment. Pali is sacred language of the earliest Buddhism (250 BCE).

According to Wikipedia, mindfulness is also practiced by Zen Buddhism (Buddhist migration to China, first century CE) called *zazen*. Zazen is a meditative discipline that is typically the primary practice of the Zen Buddhist tradition. The meaning and method of zazen varies from school to school, but in general it can be regarded as a means of insight into the nature of existence or reality. The aim of zazen is sitting, suspending all judgmental thinking, and letting words, ideas, images and thoughts pass by without getting involved in them.

A Pali language scholar, Thomas Whilian Rhys Davids (1843–1922), first translated sati in 1881 as English mindfulness. Vipassana meditation originated with a form of first-century CE Buddhism that became popular in the United States in the late 1800s. The two entities that reinvented Buddhist meditation and mindfulness were the Unitarian Church and the Theosophical Society. The Unitarian Church had a connection to scholars from India. The Theosophical Society was officially formed in New York City in 1875, which promotes Greek philosophy of third-century CE Vipassana Buddhism.

The next phase of Buddhism-based mindfulness meditation was with Jon Kabat-Zinn in 1979 in the U.S. He found the Mindfulness-Based Stress Reduction (MBSR) program at the University of Massachusetts to treat chronically ill patients.

PSYCHOLOGY OF MINDFULNESS

Psychology, especially clinical psychology since the 1970s, developed a number of therapeutic applications based on mindfulness for helping people experiencing a variety of psychological conditions. Some of these applications are anxiety, depression, drug abuse, and the psychology of pain. Mindfulness programs have been adopted in schools, prisons, hospitals, and veterans' centers for athletics, weight management, wellness, and a host of other issues.

It has been shown in clinical studies that there are benefits of mindfulness meditation in both physical and mental health. Research studies have shown that mindfulness-based interventions provide therapeutic benefits to people with psychiatric disorders, such as those with psychosis.

Rumination and worry are found in several mental disorders, including anxiety and grief. Mindfulness is perhaps the most relevant personality trait for meditation-based interventions. It refers to the innate capacity of paying attention to and maintaining attention to present-moment experiences with an open and nonjudgmental attitude. Studies have shown that trait-based mindfulness can reduce worry and rumination.

We have previously discussed how dwelling on stressful thoughts can accentuate physical health problems or cause issues with a person's physical health. Stress causes activation of the sympathetic nervous system and the hypothalamus-pituitary-adrenal axis, which can lead to physical and health-related clinical manifestations, especially in the heart and digestive tract.

Studies indicate that mindfulness meditation brings about reductions in rumination and alters these biological clinical pathways. Studies have also shown that eliminating stress improves the function of the immune system and decreases inflammation. Mindfulness meditation has been shown to improve immune function and decrease inflammation, which helps reduce diseases such as cancer and immunological diseases such as systemic lupus erythematosus.

An adverse effect can occur if too much trait-based mindfulness meditation is used. It can produce harmful effects, such as worsening anxiety in people with high levels of self-focus or awareness of their bodies or emotions.

Even though there have been clinical studies showing the benefits of mindfulness therapy, more randomized controlled studies could better document the advantages and value of mindfulness therapy. Also, mindfulness therapy has become too commercialized monetarily. This diminishes the science associated with mindfulness.

THE PRACTICE OF MINDFULNESS IN THE EARLY BUDDHISM TRADITIONS

According to Wikipedia, mindfulness as a modern, Western practice is founded on Zen and modern Vipassana, and involves the training of sati. Vipassana or *vipassana*, literally "special, super, seeing," is a Buddhist term that is often translated as "insight." The *Pali Canon* describes it as one of two qualities of mind that are developed in *bhavan*, the training of the mind, and *samatha* (mind calming). It is often defined as a practice that seeks "insight into the true nature of reality." *Anicca" impermanence," dukkha* "suffering or Un-satisfactoriness," and *anattā* "non-self" are the three marks of existence in Theravada tradition (Buddhism's oldest school or the closest teachings of Buddha). Zen Buddhism is originally from China, but it is also popular southeast Asia and Japan.

Mindfulness is included in Buddhism's Seven Factors of Enlightenment and in the Eightfold Noble Paths. The Seven Factors of Awakening are mindfulness, investigation of the nature of reality, relaxation or tranquility, energy, concentration, joy, and equanimity. The Eightfold Path consists of eight practices: right view, right resolve, right speech, right conduct, right livelihood, right effort, right mindfulness, and right meditative absorption (or Equanimeous or calm meditative awareness).

In Buddhism, the Seven Factors of Enlightenment and the Eightfold Nobel Paths are considered the pathway to the highest level. Nirvana is a transcendent state in which there is neither suffering, desire, nor sense of self, and the subject is released from the effects of karma and the cycle of death and rebirth. It represents the final goal of Buddhism. Nirvana is a state of being in which greed, hatred, and delusion have been overcome and abandoned and are absent from the mind.

CONTEMPORARY MINDFULNESS PRACTICE

Contemporary mindfulness practice involves the process of developing the skill of bringing one's attention to whatever is happening in the present moment. It is translated by some practitioners from the Buddhist practice, which considers formal and informal meditation and non-meditative practices.

Formal mindfulness meditation is the practice of sustaining attention on body, breathing sensations, use of sensory and senses, or whatever arises in each moment. Informal mindfulness is the application of mindful attention in everyday life.

The American Psychological Association (2012, defines mindfulness as "a moment-to-moment awareness of one's experience without judgment. In this sense, mindfulness is a state and not a trait. While it might be promoted by certain practices or activities, such as meditation, it is not equivalent to or synonymous with them."

The contemporary models consist of two-step and five-aggregate models. They provide steps for learning how to practice mindfulness.

The practice of mindfulness should be utilized to gradually

develop self-awareness, self-knowledge, wisdom, and gratitude. This could include understanding what is in the present moment, how various thoughts arise following input from the senses, the conditioned nature of thoughts, and other realizations. In Buddhist teachings, ultimate wisdom refers to gaining deep insight into all phenomena or "seeing things as they are."

THE HEART-BRAIN TECHNIQUE

A unique method of achieving mindfulness is the HeartMath Institute's "quick coherent heart-brain technique." There are various technique variations of the same theme, which can be found at www.heartMath.org.

Simply, one places a hand over the heart and one breathes five seconds in and out. This rhythmic breathing is done in a quiet place, and one thinks of happy thoughts or images and thoughts of gratitude.

Science Associated with Heart-Mind Meditation; Quick Coherence Technique

The autonomic nervous system is a component of the peripheral nervous system, which is connected to the brain. The autonomic nervous system regulates involuntary physiologic processes, including heart rate, blood pressure, respiration, digestion, and sexual arousal. It contains three anatomically distinct divisions: sympathetic, parasympathetic, and enteric.

Both the heart and lungs are connected to the sympathetic and parasympathetic systems. The sympathetic raises heart rate and rapid breathing, and the parasympathetic calms the heart rate and breathing. Both are also involved in the fight-or-flight response, which is a sympathetic response. This response is associated with stress, anger, and worry.

The limbic system in the brain is made up of the cingulate gyrus, parahippocampal gyrus, amygdala, hypothalamus, insula, and hippocampus. The limbic system is the part of the brain involved in human behavioral and emotional responses. It is especially involved in human behaviors concerned with survival: feelings/emotions, reproduction, caring for young, and fight-or-flight responses.

The amygdala is commonly thought to form the core of a neural system for processing fearful and threatening stimuli, including detection of threats and activation of appropriate fear-related behaviors in response to threatening or dangerous stimuli. It is also involved with negative emotions, including stress, anxiety, anger, sadness, nervousness, disgust, and loneliness. It can also be involved with joy and happiness. Happiness activates several areas of the brain, including the right frontal cortex, the precuneus, the left amygdala, and the left insula. This activity involves connections between awareness (frontal cortex and insula) and the "feeling center" (amygdala) of the brain.

With the parasympathetic nervous system and the help of the hypothalamus-pituitary-adrenal (HPA) axis, the amygdala, and the prefrontal cortex, we can calm ourselves during stressful situations.

THE HEART-BRAIN CONNECTION

In medicine, we are taught that the brain has a major effect on the heart. This is true when it comes to fight-or-flight reactions. The sympathetic nervous system is connected to the heart to stimulate increased heart rate. The heart has a major impact on the brain. The heart has a strong electromagnetic field and is strongly connected to the parasympathetic nervous system that travels back to the brain, allowing for decreased heart rate and decreased breathing. The parasympathetic system comes into play after a fight-or-flight response.

Stimulation of the parasympathetic nervous system produces calming of the brain's amygdala and the hypothalamus-pituitary-adrenal axis. The heart can have an impact on this system, according to the HeartMath Institute. They found that erratic electrical activity in the heart due to stress leads to poor cognitive function in the brain, and stable activity leads to calming effects in the brain. The erratic electromagnetic field is associated with the parasympathetic nervous system, and orderly and stable activity is associated with the parasympathetic nervous system.

Breathing has an effect on heart rate and pulse transit time. It has been shown that ten-second rhythm achieves positive effects on the heart (five seconds on the in breath and five seconds on the out breath). Breathing rhythmically in this fashion can be a useful intervention to initiate a shift out of a stressful emotional state and into increased coherence.

Measurement of heart rate variability, blood pressure rhythm (pulse transit time), and respiration rhythm can be used for sympathetic and parasympathetic activity. When all of them are out of synchronization, it indicates stress; a harmonious and synchronized pattern is called coherence. When the quick coherence technique is used, the heart causes a parasympathetic response. This causes stress reduction.

The coherence of the heart and breathing sends signals to the limbic system, especially the amygdala. By establishing coherence of heart-breathing synchronization on a regular basis with the quick cohesive technique, the amygdala and limbic system are readjusted to reduce stress.

THE AUTHOR'S OWN TECHNIQUES

A very helpful technique that I use is to fill the bathtub with warm water and add lavender to the water. Lying on my back in the water, my head is immersed to cover my ears. A hand is placed over my heart. Deep rhythmical breathing is maintained. I can hear my own breathing and heartbeat. With deep rhythmical breathing, the water moves like waves. Thinking peaceful, positive thoughts should take place.

In this truly mindful setting, you can feel the warmth of the water, smell the lavender, hear breathing and heart sounds, and feel the water moving up and down with the diaphragm. This totally forces one to be mindful. Body, mind, and awareness completes all the senses except taste, and you can place peppermint in your mouth to experience taste. This is a real moment-by-moment experience. You can even feel the change in water temperature over time.

Another technique is more meditative: using the HeartMath technique while listening to New Age music.

Mindfulness SELF MEASUREMENT Tests

There are several tests one can take to evaluate how attentive one is to being mindful.

MINDFULNESS TESTING EVALUATIONS

THE MINDFUL ATTENTION AWARENESS SCALE (MAAS)

The MAAS is a fifteen-item scale that is designed to assess a core characteristic of mindfulness, a receptive state of mind in which attention, informed by a sensitive awareness of what is occurring in the present, simply observes what is taking place. This is a good test for self-awareness.

The Freiburg Mindfulness Inventory (FMI) is a fifteen-item questionnaire that measures mindfulness with a score of 1–4. This is an easy questionnaire to take and accurate when answered truthfully.

The Cognitive and Affective Mindfulness Scale (CAMS) is a ten-item test that measures self-awareness accurately. It evaluates acceptance, judgment, and awareness.

The Five-Facet Mindfulness Questionnaire (FFMQ) has thirty-nine questions on observing describing, acting with awareness, and nonjudging of inner experience and non-reactivity to inner experience. The last two examine self-esteem to some extent.

All of these are self-reporting. They are very accurate. I took each test and scored the same on each one. The Five-Facet Mindfulness

Questionnaire is the most complete one. They all measure body-mind awareness. One can even include perception while taking the tests.

MINDFULNESS THERAPY IN CLINICAL PSYCHOLOGY

Buddhist mindfulness has creeped into modern psychology in many forms and therapeutic methodologies in clinical psychology. We are noting a few of the several applications.

MINDFULNESS-BASED STRESS REDUCTION (MBSR)

MBSR was one of the first techniques or mindfulness-based program developed by Jon Kabat-Zinn in 1979 at the University of Massachusetts Medical Center. His method uses a combination of mindfulness meditation, body awareness, and yoga to help people become more mindful and reduce stress. While MBSR has its roots in spiritual teachings, the program itself is secular.

MINDFULNESS-BASED COGNITIVE THERAPY (MBCT)

MBCT is considered psychological therapy for relapses of depression for people with major depressive disorder. MBCT uses traditional cognitive behavioral therapy methods and adds newer psychological strategies, such as mindfulness and mindfulness meditation. Cognitive methods can include educating the participant about depression.

Mindfulness and mindfulness meditation focus on becoming aware of all incoming thoughts and feelings and accepting them—but not attaching or reacting to them. The goal of MBCT is to interrupt negative automatic processes and teach the participants to focus less on reacting to incoming negative thoughts by accepting and observing them without judgment. This mindfulness practice allows the participant to notice when automatic negative processes are occurring and to alter their reactions to be more like reflections. Research supports the effects of MBCT in people who have been depressed three or more times and demonstrates reduced relapse rates by 50 percent.

ACCEPTANCE AND COMMITMENT THERAPY (ACT)

ACT is a form of clinical behavioral analysis that is used in psychotherapy as an intervention that uses acceptance and mindfulness strategies mixed in different ways with commitment and behavior-change strategies to increase flexibility

DIALECTICAL BEHAVIOR THERAPY (DBT)

Mindfulness is a core exercise that is used in dialectical behavior therapy. DBT is a form of treatment for people with borderline personality disorders. DBT is reconciliation of opposites in a continual process of synthesis.

MOVING ON IN LIFE

Merriam-Webster defines moving on in life as "to continue living one's life in the usual way after all the problems they've had recently." When one moves on in life, it is usually in the form of perseverance when the right choice is made. Perseverance is persistence in doing something despite difficulty.

Moving on is a frequently used term in relationships. When a close relationship ends, people often say, "It's time to move on!" Moving on in grief is similar. Usually, it is said by other people around the grieving person. It generally means to stop hurting, stop talking about it, stop crying, stop remembering, stop grieving, and so forth. Others want the hurting person to stop grieving because they don't want to feel the pain. It is not a happy experience for either person. The grieving person frequently becomes isolated by others, yet part of the healing process is to be with and talk to others. It's a catch-22. It becomes a choice for the grieving person to choose empathetic persons to talk to about grief.

Acceptance means that the pain is dissipating or has gone away. That doesn't mean forgetting. Moving on means one has moved from pain to acceptance.

Mental or emotional pain associated with grief is complex. Each person has their own timeline with the grieving process, but acceptance is considered the end of the grieving process. However, we think moving on in life should be the last phase of grieving.

Moving on in life occurs after acceptance. It is a period of choices. The choice is to extend one's life in fear, anxiety, or depression or move on with life as before the loss. The latter means living a full and happy life even as one continues to miss what one lost—whether it is a loved one or something personal.

They must now think in terms of their own life and what is next for them. One can think of moving on with life like a disaster. If your house burns down, one can keep it in ashes or rebuild it, which is moving on with life. That doesn't mean losing everything is easy, but there are memories—and that is not forgetting.

SUMMARY

Acceptance in the grieving process is the last stage of Elizabeth Kübler-Ross's five stages of grief. We added shock as the first stage and moving on as the last stage; therefore, shock, denial, anger, bargaining, depression, acceptance, and moving on. These stages do not always occur in order. One may only go through a few stages. For example, when I was diagnosed with stage 4 colon cancer in 2000, I went from denial to moving on and skipped all the other stages.

GRIEF, FORGIVENESS, ACCEPTANCE, AND REJECTION

This chapter also evaluates methods for accomplishing acceptance. Some of the emotions in grief are anxiety and depression. Mindfulness training can overcome some of the negative aspects of grief and help achieve acceptance. Counseling with therapy can also help to overcome grief, lead to acceptance, and help with moving on.

CHAPTER 5
SOCIAL ACCEPTANCE AND REJECTION BY OTHER PEOPLE

> "No person is your friend who demands your
> silence, or denies your right to grow.
> —Alice Walker

Social acceptance is extremely complex, and it is more complex than self-acceptance. It includes acceptance by peers and groups. It involves political, religious, gender, sexual, environmental, technological, and many more types and forms of acceptance. In this context, one can easily appreciate the complexity of social acceptance. The term social acceptance has dual meanings: one where a person accepts others (chapter 6) and one where a person is accepted by others (this chapter).

Social acceptance can be divided into internal and external acceptance; internal is the ability to accept others, and external is when other individuals or groups accept an individual.

Social acceptance by others is defined as the degree to which an individual is actively brought into social interactions by others in individual and/or group relationships. Barriers to social acceptance may include prejudice or stigma. It means that other people signal that they wish to include you in their groups and relationships. Social acceptance occurs on a continuum that ranges from merely tolerating another person's presence to actively creating long-lasting relationships or friends. Social acceptance affects people of all social and age groups.

Social acceptance of others can be defined as tolerating the differences and diversity in others because most people attempt to look and act like others do in order to fit in.

Psychologists have an overall definition of social acceptance. Social acceptance means that other people signal that they wish to include a person in their group or relationships. Social acceptance should occur on a continuous basis to provide positive feelings. This may range from tolerating another person to actively pursuing a permanent relationship.

SOCIAL ACCEPTANCE BY OTHER PEOPLE

Social acceptance is associated with self-esteem and well-being. There is a fundamental need for positive and lasting relationships, which is at the core of human soul. Acceptance by others and self-acceptance are major components of self-esteem.

Social acceptance is not unique to humans. Most animals live in groups, and there is social acceptance within the group. It is also found with fish, birds, and many other species. It is a means of survival and procreation to extend life. Acceptance by the mother in animals is critical for survival; if rejected, a newborn will not survive. Creating strong offspring from the beginning increases survival. Weak offspring are prone to disease and predators. Acceptance at birth is extremely important for survival and building strong offspring, both physically and mentally.

The male or father plays a secondary role, but acceptance of the offspring creates strong and physically and mentally healthy offspring.

In humans, parental bonding is so important for creating self-esteem. Positive, loving, and supportive bonding establishes the bond. Positive reinforcement throughout childhood into the teenage years provides good mental health. Strong acceptance is extremely important. Embarrassment, scorn, apathy, and rejection toward a child can cause diminished self-esteem and self-worth. Emotional distress from social disapproval can lead to anxiety and depression in the form of doubt, neglect, distress, and nervousness. Approval, support, and love from others will strengthen confidence, self-worth, and well-being. Girls are more sensitive to the distresses than boys. An excellent example is social media, which has created negative feedback for girls when peers disapprove of one another.

Children and teenagers desire to be accepted among friends as part of that group. As a result, they act upon that desire through peer pressure. Peer pressure frequently determines behavior and appearance. The values of the group determine behavior because the child or teenager wants to fit in. These are the years where we see positive activities with a group, such as sports or playing in a band or negative activities, such as smoking cigarettes, swearing, or drinking alcohol.

In adults, social acceptance relies on the needs within the group, even if the individuals are individualistic. The need for social acceptance lies within the social cohesiveness of society. Social belonging is dependent on the responsibility of each person to contribute to the group. Those who want to enhance their chances of inclusion are frequently motivated to maintain social approval.

The need for social approval is affected by developmental stages, racial and cultural factors, type and nature of society, generational influences, and inherent characteristics and traits of the individual.

Group dynamics play an important role in individual behavior. A group that is accepting and open to individualism has higher sociability than a group that is restrictive or regimented, which may lead to isolation.

Every human being has a fundamental need for positive and lasting relationships. However, it is unfortunate that rejection by others frequently exists as well. Like acceptance, rejection is also a complex issue. It consists of behaviors that can range from ignoring another person's presence to actively expelling them from a group or existing relationship. In extreme situations, it could even be physical.

Wikipedia defines social rejection as occurring when an individual is deliberately excluded from a social relationship or social interaction.

Rejection can come from parents to children, peers, spouses, and so forth. Rejection includes bullying, ridiculing, and slandering, and it can be passive by ignoring or talking badly to others. Most mammals are social, but in humans, there is a level of rejection. It becomes a real problem when rejection is prolonged and persistent.

The responses a person feels from social rejection are emotional, cognitive, behavioral, biological, and neural. In terms of emotional responses, social rejection tends to increase negative emotions. The psychological consequences are isolation, loneliness, low self-esteem, aggression, anxiety, and depression. There is heightened sensitivity to negativity and rejection. Insecurity can also occur. The psychological consequences can lead to poor physical health, such as insomnia, weight gain or loss, heart disease, or even cancer.

According to studies, minimal contact is not enough to create and maintain mental health. Emotional contact with a caring and loving nature is necessary. People need stable relationships and satisfying interactions with the people in those relationships. If any of the two are missing, a person feels rejection, loneliness, and unhappiness.

Belonging to a group is important for social identification, self-concept, and self-identity. Fear of rejection can lead to being influenced by the demands of others and peer pressure.

CHILDHOOD REJECTION BY OTHERS

Whether intentional or unintentional, being rejected by one parent or both can be mentally devastating. The result is often low self-esteem, chronic insecurity, anxiety, and depression. Often the impact lasts well into adulthood. They might even develop hostility and aggression toward others. This doesn't end in childhood, and the emotional pain lingers into adulthood.

The causes for parental rejection are many. Rarely, it is mental disease by the mother, although postpartum depression in women with no prior history of depression is 12 percent. This can persist, which can cause rejection of the baby and persistent childhood rejection. Severe mental health issues in the mother or father are another risk factor.

Commonly, the cause is dysfunction between the parents. They may not even be cognizant of their rejection of the child because they are involved with their own issues.

Much of the mental health of a child is dependent upon a functional relationship between the parents. Forced marriages and having children can cause rejection of the child. A common cause is related to a child born from an affair, a secret to all except the mother who feels guilt every time she sees the child. A rape can also cause rejection. Despite good intentions, it is difficult to put aside the past.

Divorce is a double-edged sword for the mental health of a child. Divorce can lead to feelings of abandonment. Unhappy parents who don't get a divorce because of religious reasons, pressure from family, or economic challenges might blame the child for keeping them locked in a loveless relationship.

Teenage pregnancies can also create a substantial problem with rejection. A family member, usually the mother of the teenager, might attempt to raise the child. The situation becomes dire when the child of the teenager is never told about their biological mother—and the teenage mother is treated as a sister.

Unconscious rejection of child may occur when the parent has been rejected or abused as a child.

There is nothing more cruel or immoral than forcing a woman to bear a child that is not wanted. No matter what the circumstances may be, nothing is more morally outrageous than forced birth from rape or incest. This leads to rejection of the child, which causes severe mental health issues that can lead to violence.

A case in point is the school shooting in Uvalde Texas. On May 24, 2022, nineteen students and two teachers were fatally shot—and seventeen others were wounded. Earlier in the day, eighteen-year-old

Salvador Ramos shot his grandmother in the head. It was reported that he struggled with mental health as a result of parental rejection.

Christian conservatives and the Christian right helped overturn *Roe v. Wade* to criminalize abortions and prevent any abortions—even in cases of rape and incest—in many Republican states. This creates more mental health issues in children who are unwanted. Many Republicans refuse to acknowledge mental health problems in the United States and provide no funding for mental health. Therefore, we can expect more school shootings since Republicans refuse to do anything about gun control.

PEER REJECTION

Peer rejection is also a problem for children. Peer rejection is a global term that encompasses the many behaviors used by children to exclude and hurt one another, including overt forms of control and harm. Children who experience rejection have problems sharing and taking turns. They have higher rates of disruption, aggression, and impulsive behaviors. In addition, they have higher rates of social anxiety.

Studies show that minority children, children with disabilities, and children who have unusual characteristics or behaviors face greater risk of rejection. Obviously, well-liked children show social intelligence and know when and how to join playgroups as small children and cliquish groups as teenagers.

Rejected children are more likely to be bullied. Negative behaviors against rejected children do not go away and are quite harmful. Studies show that a rejected child who transfers to another school maintains the same stigma of rejection. This shows that social groups and social stigma are stable.

Internalization becomes a real risk in rejected children, including depression, suicidal ideation, and suicide. Internalization means an individual's acceptance of a set of norms and/or values through socialization. Rejection can lead to negative internalization.

Peer rejection can lead to school shootings. A study analyzing fifteen school shootings between 1995 and 2001 found that peer rejection was present in all but two of the cases (87 percent).[6] Bullying was one of the main features of the rejection. Depression, isolation, and poor impulse control were also present.

Can school socialization programs reverse peer rejection? Some school programs help children who suffer from rejection. A meta-analysis study reviewed 79 controlled studies and found that social skills training is statistically very effective with a 70 percent success rate, compared to 30 percent success in control groups.[7]

ADULT REJECTION BY OTHERS

OSTRACISM

Ostracism is exclusion from a society or group of people. Kipling Williams, a social psychologist, defines ostracism as "any act or acts of ignoring and excluding of an individual or groups by an individual or a group" without necessarily involving "acts of verbal or physical abuse."

We think of ostracism in terms of it occurring in adults rather than children due to the origin of the word. Ostracism was a Greek democratic procedure in which any citizen could be expelled from the city or state of Athens for ten years.

Ostracism also occurs in the animal kingdom and arose in primitive human societies. It can lead to death due to the lack of protection and access to food resources. Therefore, living within a group or society provides survival of the genetic line, and ostracizing an individual prevents procreation. On the other hand, ostracism has

---

[6] Leary, M. R.; Kowalski, R. M.; Smith, L. (2003). "Teasing, rejection, and violence: Case studies of the school shootings." *Aggressive Behavior*. 29 (3): 202–214. doi:10.1002/ab.10061.

[7] Schneider, B. H. (1992). "Didactic methods for enhancing children's peer relations: A quantitative review." *Clinical Psychology Review*. 12 (3): 363–382. doi:10.1016/0272-.

been used by animal species to strengthen the species by eliminating weak, noncontributing, or nonconforming members.

Social psychologists propose that ostracism poses a threat to four fundamental human needs: the need to belong, the need for control in social situations, the need to maintain high levels of self-esteem, and the need to have a sense of a meaningful existence. Lacking any or all of these needs leads to mental distress and psychological pain.

How fast does a person respond to even the minor ostracism, such as being ignored? It is as fast as a reflex. When the doctor taps a knee, the leg jerks. As soon as the patella is tapped with a reflex hammer, a message is sent to the spinal cord and returns with the leg jerking in a matter of milliseconds. The reaction when someone is ignored is also in milliseconds, which is precognitive. This all takes place in the same regions of the brain as experiencing physical pain. Research has shown the activated regions of the brain during a brief episode of minimal ostracism include the dorsal anterior cingulate cortex. Researchers have also discovered that the regions of the brain associated with emotions also affect the pain regions.

In medical management of physical pain, doctors have known for some time that emotions affect physical pain because serotonin reuptake inhibitors used for depression, such as Cymbalta, also decrease physical pain.

The immediate mechanisms associated with ostracism are both adaptive and a means for survival. A person who is ostracized usually goes through a reflective stage to determine their response to the exclusion. If it is meaningless, despite the immediate pain response, the person can ignore the exclusion. More painful situations require coping. Coping with ostracism can cause a variety of responses. One can reestablish self-esteem by trying to behave in ways that will meet the group's approval or by joining a new group or changing interests, such as golfing to tennis. One could gain recognition in a national or international group, which could force recognition with the local group that was participating in ostracism. Control could be done through aggression or violence, but this is usually a form of terminal acceptance into the group.

CANCEL CULTURE

The public shaming of those deemed moral transgressors is an age-old social phenomenon. Cancel culture is a modern form of ostracism in which someone is thrust out of social or professional circles—whether it is online, on social media, or in person. Those who are subject to this ostracism are said to have been "canceled"[8] The expression "cancel culture" has mostly negative connotations and is commonly used in debates on free speech and censorship.

A term that is also used is call-out culture, which is defined as a way of behaving in a society or group in which people are often criticized in public—for example, on social media—for their words or actions or are asked to explain to them. It is often associated with boycotting or shunning an individual, usually a celebrity, who has acted or spoken in an unacceptable manner. Some believe cancel culture has a negative effect or discrimination of free speech, but others argue that cancel culture is a form of free speech. The cancel culturalism group also argues for accountability and consequences.

Merriam-Webster states that to "cancel" means "to stop giving support to [a] person."

Dictionary.com defines cancel culture as "withdrawing support for (canceling) public figures and companies after they have done or said something considered objectionable or offensive."

In a 2021 report, Eric Kaufmann characterized cancel culture in academia as a form of "hard authoritarianism" involving "no-platforming, dismissal campaigns, social media mob attacks, open letters, and formal complaints and disciplinary action."[9]

Ostracism threatens individuals' psychological and physical well-being. Ostracizing behaviors can be subtle (averted gaze) or overt (being completely nonresponsive to the person's presence).

Discrimination is the unjust or prejudicial treatment of different

---

[8] Buchanan, Larry; Bui, Quoctrung; Patel, Jugal K. (July 3, 2020). *New York Times*.
[9] Ibid.

categories of people or things, especially on the grounds of race, age, or sex.

Prejudice is a preconceived opinion that is not based on reason or actual experience or harm or injury that results from an action or judgment.

Censorship is the suppression or prohibition of any parts of books, films, news, and so forth that are considered obscene, politically unacceptable, or a threat to security.

Free speech is the right to express an opinion without censorship or restraint. Freedom of speech, protected by the First and Fourteenth Amendments to the U.S. Constitution, which expresses information, ideas, and opinions on freedom of speech. Some of the limits to freedom of speech are incitement, defamation, fraud, obscenity, child pornography, fighting words, and threats.

The attitudes and behaviors of those who indulge in cancel culture include hostility, stalking, intimidation, harassment, vigilantism, a holier than thou attitude, prejudice, and discrimination. People have been publicly denounced for their wrongdoing throughout history, and there is supporting documentation in the Bible.

The Bible has several verses that apply to cancel culture two thousand years ago:

> Do not pervert justice; do not show partiality to the poor or favoritism to the great, but judge your neighbor fairly. (Leviticus 19:15 NIV)

> Take no part in the unfruitful works of darkness, but instead expose them. (Ephesians 5:11 NIV)

Cancel culture originated from the term canceled, and being called out become popular in cancel culture.

In 1981, Nile Rodgers wrote "Your Love Is Canceled" after a really bad date with a woman who wanted to use his celebrity status for her favor. Barry Michael Cooper referred to women being canceled in his 1991 film *New Jack City*. The term also became popular in African-American vernacular.

With social media, cancel culture became a common term. It has been tagged to liberals, but conservatives use the phrase frequently.

"Call-out culture" has been in use since 2014 as part of the #MeToo movement.

#MeToo is a social movement against abuse of women, including sexual abuse, sexual harassment, and rape culture. People publicize their experiences of sexual abuse or sexual harassment. The movement encouraged women (and men) to call out their abusers on a forum where the accusations would be heard, especially against very powerful individuals.

Call-out culture has also been promoted by the black community with Black Lives Matter. Cancel culture gained popularity in 2019 as society demanded accountability for offensive conduct. Most cancel culture occurs in the media. It became a talking point on late-night talk shows. It was discussed frequently on HBO's *Bill Maher Show* as he questioned the liberals and free speech.

Cancel culture is not a term of just liberals, but rather conservatives have also engaged in the use of the phrase. They have misused the term for those who use politically incorrect speech.

What is the difference between collegial criticism and a harmful response to something said or done by another person? What is the psychological health of the person calling out another? What is free speech, thought control, and suppression of speech?

Cancel culture is a childish form of name-calling. It is not a form of collegial criticism, which would lead to an intellectual and knowledgeable debate. It is more like verbal bullying. As such, a person initiates and habitually seeks to harm or intimidate those they perceive as vulnerable. And the higher up the person is in society, the more severe the results.

Cancel culture would not have any prominence if it were not for social media. Social media allows for meme crowd theory, which is like rapid cellular replication. In a matter of minutes, hundreds and thousands of viewers can see someone, like a comedian, who has been canceled for using a slur. Cancel culture would not readily have a crowd in agreement with the leader. The individual leader serves as a self-policing person of public figures or companies after they have done or said something objectionable or offensive.

Media scholars describe cancel culture as a collective of typically marginalized voices emphatically expressing their own censure of a powerful person. Since social media, such as Facebook, has limited censorship, the culture has no control other than to fight back on social media.

Despite all the hoopla, cancel culture has no positive outcomes. It's nihilistic since nothing is corrected by its practice. It may produce an action of forgiveness or an apology. However, for the most part, it is ineffective. Society is quick to pass judgment against those they view as public offenders or personae non grata. The practice contributes to the polarization of American society, but it does not lead to changes in opinion.

However, calling someone out can have a positive effect and create change. It is apparent that the context and process of calling out is effective.

RESPONSES TO CANCEL CULTURE

The responses to cancel culture have mostly been expressed as negative, and it is commonly used in debates about free speech and censorship. Responses have come from presidents, historians, TV hosts, and public opinion.

Barack Obama warned against social media call-out culture and said, "People who do really good stuff have flaws. People who you are fighting may love their kids and, you know, share certain things with you." Donald Trump also criticized cancel culture in a speech in July 2020, comparing it to totalitarianism and claiming that it is a political weapon used to punish and shame dissenters by driving them from their jobs and demanding submission. Obviously, he did not understand the concept of cancel culture in his speech.

Bill Maher and others have blamed cancel culture on liberals, but historian David Olusegun disagrees. He states that for the past forty years, right-wing newspapers, motivated by financial and political ambitions, have ceaselessly fought to delegitimize and ultimately cancel the BBC.

The Hill took a poll about attitudes toward cancel culture. A total of 46 percent of registered voters surveyed agreed that cancel culture "has gone too far," and 10 percent said it has not gone far enough. Another 18 percent said it has neither gone too far nor not far enough, and slightly more than a quarter of respondents, 26 percent, said they didn't know or didn't have an opinion.

The survey defined "cancel culture" using dictionary.com's definition: "the practice of withdrawing support for (or canceling) public figures and companies after they have done or said something considered objectionable or offensive."

Nearly half of respondents, 49 percent, said they believe cancel culture has had a negative effect on society, while 27 percent said they think it has had a positive impact. And 40 percent responded that they have participated in cancel culture, and about 1 in 10 said they participate in it "often."

About half of Democrats and a third of Republicans reported that they shared their disapproval of a public figure on social media after the figure did something controversial. Age also plays a factor, according to the poll, with Gen Z and millennials being most likely to approve of cancel culture, while Gen Xers and baby boomers are more likely to disapprove. A total of 55 percent of voters ages eighteen to thirty-four reported participating in cancel culture, while 32 percent of voters over 65 said the same.

Respondents' disapproval of a public figure also depended on when their public statements were made. For those from a year ago, 54 percent said a controversial statement would "completely" or "somewhat" change their opinion of the individual, while 29 percent said it would "change a little bit" or "not change at all."

For statements from fifteen years ago or more, that breakdown flipped: 26 percent said the statement would "completely" or "somewhat" change their opinion, while 53 percent reported it would "change a little bit" or "not change at all."

A March 2021 poll by the Harvard Center for American Political Studies and the Harris Poll found that 64 percent of respondents viewed "a growing cancel culture" as a threat to their freedom, while the other 36 percent did not. And 36 percent of respondents said that cancel culture is a big problem, 32 percent called it a moderate problem, 20 percent called it a small problem, and 13 percent said it is not a problem. And 54 percent said they were concerned that if they expressed their opinions online, they would be banned or fired, while the other 46 percent said they were not concerned.[10]

CONSEQUENCES

What are the consequences for those who are canceled? We can go back two thousand years and see what the Bible tells us about being canceled.

> Do not show partiality in judging; hear both small and great alike. Do not be afraid of anyone, for judgment belongs to God. Bring me any case too hard for you, and I will hear it. (Deuteronomy 1:17 NIV)

There are people who would like to change the term cancel culture to consequence culture. Consequence is defined as a result or effect of an action or condition. The terms have different connotations. Cancel culture focuses on the effect, and discussion is limited by a desire to maintain a certain viewpoint; consequence culture focuses on the idea that those who write or publish opinions or make statements should bear some responsibility for the effects of these on people.[11]

---

[10] https://thehill.com/homenews/news/508527-poll-plurality-of-voters-say-cancel-culture-has-gone-too-far/.

[11] https://caps.gov.harvard.edu/caps-harris-poll.

The consequences affect the cancelers and those who have been canceled. Both parties have a responsibility, and both have some degree of consequences.

A simple slip or blunder could be referring to a man's daughter as his mistress. If this was done over some form of media the person who made the comment may be canceled. This may result in an apology. More serious issues usually result in resignations, terminations, or lawsuits.

In February 2021, science and health reporter Donald McNeil Jr. resigned from the *New York Times* after facing criticism for repeating a racial slur in a 2019 conversation about a student being suspended for saying an unacceptable word.

Being called out led to the resignation of the head coach of the Las Vegas Raiders. On October 11, 2021, the *New York Times* reported that John Gruden sent emails using homophobic, racist, and sexist language. The emails were uncovered as part of the National Football League's investigation into workplace misconduct allegations against the Washington Football Team. The emails occurred ten years ago, and some were addressed to the team president, Bruce Allen. Gruden reportedly called Roger Goodell, NFL commissioner, a "fa***t" and "clueless anti football p****y" in those emails. This led to the former coach filing a lawsuit against the NFL and Roger Goodell, ruining Gruden's career. The consequences led to a lot of consternation in football, which is a sport that uses all sorts of bad language. Goodell has contended that Gruden denounced the emergence of women as referees, the drafting of a gay player, and the tolerance of players protesting during the playing of the National Anthem.

The state of Florida passed Parental Rights in Education Law, which opponents have derisively nicknamed "Don't Say Gay" legislation. Walt Disney, Co. spoke out against and publicly condemned the law, which caused a reflex canceled out response from Governor DeSantis. On April 24, 2022, Governor Ron DeSantis rescinded a fifty-five-year-old special district, giving the company self-governing powers around Walt Disney World, saving Florida taxpayers billions of dollars. When the governor canceled the contract, the taxpayers had to come up with the money. This led to a lawsuit by Disney against Florida because of free speech, which is based on the First Amendment.

FREEDOM OF SPEECH

We like to call freedom of speech acceptance of speech since it falls under social acceptance. Acceptance of speech places a qualitative and quantitative measure on speech, whereas freedom of speech is more legalistic.

It is clear that cancel culture falls under free speech. Freedom of speech is the right to express any opinion without consequences, restraint, or censorship. Freedom of speech is considered a principle that supports individual, group, or community freedom to articulate opinions and ideas without fear of retaliation, censorship, or legal sanctions. Freedom of speech falls under the First Amendment of the United States Constitution. This is not to be confused with the freedom of expression.

Freedom of expression has been recognized as a human right in the Universal Declaration of Human Rights, an international human rights law, by the United Nations. Article 19 of the 1948 Universal Declaration of Human Rights states that "everyone shall have the right to hold opinions without interference" and "everyone shall have the right to freedom of expression; this right shall include freedom to seek, receive, and impart information and ideas of all kinds, regardless of frontiers, either orally, in writing or in print, in the form of art, or through any other media of his choice."

Freedom of speech and freedom of expression have limitations that include libel, slander, obscenity, child pornography, sedition, incitement, fighting words, hate speech, classified information, copyright violations, trade secrets, food labels, nondisclosure agreements, the right to privacy, the right to dignity, the right to be forgotten, public security, and perjury.

The idea of the "offense principle" (or what we call acceptance of speech) is also used to justify speech limitations. The principle describes the restriction on forms of expression deemed offensive to society, taking into account factors such as context, extent, duration, motives of the speaker, and ease with which it could be avoided. With the rise of social media, the offensive principle and acceptance of speech, and to a greater extent, illegal speech, such as hate speech is ignored.

The internet has been the cause for a revolution of censorship and free speech. Freedom of expression applies freedom of speech to any medium, and that includes the internet. Has there been any form of censorship for the internet? The Communications Decency Act of 1996 was the first major attempt by the United States Congress to regulate pornographic material on the internet. This act was overturned in 1997 by the Supreme Court, allowing for freedom of expression for adults.

There is language on the internet, especially social media, that surely tests the limits of conventional discourse. Speech on the internet can be unfiltered, disgusting, emotionally charged, sexually explicit, and vulgar—in a word, "indecent" in many communities. Of course, this is to be expected when people from all socioeconomic groups have access with a computer or smartphone.

The World Summit on the Information Society Declaration of Principles adopted in 2003 makes specific reference to the importance of the right to freedom of expression for the Information Society:

> We reaffirm, as an essential foundation of the Information society, and as outlined in Article 19 of the Universal Declaration of Human Rights, that everyone has the right to freedom of opinion and expression; that this right includes freedom to hold opinions without interference and to seek, receive and impart information and ideas through any media and regardless of frontiers. Communication is a fundamental social process, a basic human need and the foundation of all social organization. It is central

to the Informational Society. Everyone, everywhere should have the opportunity to participate and no one should be excluded from the benefits of the Information Society offers.

The Republican Party has tried to censor or eliminate information in public schools regard gender, race, and sex education. They have tried to eliminate Google, National Public Radio, and the Public Broadcasting Service. It would appear Article 19 would prohibit such actions. It is unclear why incitement, fighting words, and hate speech are considered violations of free speech but are permitted on social media platforms.

Certainly cancel culture is considered free speech on the part of the person or groups and on the part of those canceling the culprits, but only when it causes pain and suffering is it a violation of freedom of speech.

John Stuart Mill (1806–73) was the most influential English philosopher of the nineteenth century. He was a naturalist, a utilitarian, and a liberal, and his work explores the consequences of a thoroughgoing empiricist outlook. *On Liberty* suggests that "the only purpose for which power can be rightfully exercised over any member of a civilized community, against his will, is to prevent harm to others."

> All things whatsoever ye would that men should do
> to you, do ye even so to them. (Matthew 7:12 KJV)

Mosaic Law—the ancient Law of the Hebrews, ascribed to Moses) contains a parallel commandment: "Whatever is hurtful to you, do not do to any other person." Only say to others what you would want them to say to you!

SUMMARY

Social acceptance has been defined as the degree to which an individual is actively brought into social interactions by others in individual and/or group relationships.

Acceptance by parents is the first stage in self-acceptance. Positive acceptance by parents leads to self-esteem in the child. This usually leads to acceptance by peers. Everyone wants some form of acceptance; as human beings, that is part of our existence. Rejection at any of the early stages can lead to mental health issues. However, when mental health issues arise, self-help in the form of meditation, prayer, and other techniques can be helpful.

The psychosocial issues involved with adult rejection are problematic, which becomes apparent as we explore ostracism and cancel culture.

CHAPTER 6
SOCIAL ACCEPTANCE AND REJECTION OF OTHER PEOPLE

> The second is this: "You shall love your neighbor as yourself."
> There is no other commandment greater than these.
> —Mark 12:31 (ESV)

> We love because he first loved us. If anyone says, "I love God," and hates his brother, he is a liar; for he who does not love his brother whom he has seen cannot love God whom he has not seen. And this commandment we have from him: whoever loves God must also love his brother.
> —1 John 4:19–21 (ESV)

Acceptance of others is the ability to see that others have a right to be their own unique persons. That means having a right to their own feelings, thoughts, and opinions. When we accept people for who they are, we let go of our desire to change them.

Merriam-Webster defines accepting others when able or willing to accept someone or to regard someone with acceptance rather than with hostility or fear. It is also tending to regard different types of people and ways of life with tolerance and acceptance.

Tolerance is a key component of accepting others. It means accepting other people's opinions and preferences—even when they live in a way that we do not agree with.

INNER CIRCLE OF ACCEPTING OTHERS

The inner circle of accepting others consists of those people closest to a person. These people are usually friends, acquaintances, family, significant others, mates, or coworkers. It is obvious why family is in this circle, but what brings two people together as friends or lovers? Personalities play a large role in close acceptance.

Accepting others into the inner circle is possibly totally dependent on personality. Common interests, intellect, cultural and religious similarities, and so forth determine how one person accepts another.

The dictionary definition of personality is the combination of characteristics or qualities that form an individual's distinctive character.

The American Psychological Association states, "Personality refers to individual differences in characteristic patterns of thinking, feeling and behaving."

According to Wikipedia, personality is the characteristic sets of behaviors, cognitions, and emotional patterns that are formed from biological and environmental factors, and which change over time.

Some psychologists define personality in terms of traits. Personality traits reflect people's characteristic patterns of thoughts, feelings, and behaviors. Personality traits imply consistency and stability—someone who scores high on a specific trait like extroversion is expected to be sociable in different situations and over time. Extroverted behaviors include being talkative, assertive, adventurous, and outgoing. Thus, trait psychology rests on the idea that people differ from one another in terms of where they stand on a set of basic trait dimensions that persist over time and across situations.

PERSONALITY DEVELOPMENT

The study of personality development is complex and difficult. The most widely used system of traits is called the Five-Factor Model. This system includes five broad traits that can be remembered with the acronym OCEAN: openness, conscientiousness, extroversion, agreeableness, and neuroticism. Each of the major traits from the Big Five can be divided into facets to give a more fine-tuned analysis of someone's personality. In addition, some trait theorists argue that there are other traits that cannot be completely captured by the Five-Factor Model. Critics of the trait concept argue that people do not act consistently from one situation to the next and are very influenced by situational forces. Thus, one major debate in the field concerns the relative power of people's traits versus the situations in which they find themselves as predictors of their behavior.

Biological developmental and environmental factors appear to influence personality. Biological factors in personality are based on the makeup of areas in the brain and the networks that are present. We have already discussed the fight-or-flight response to harm. Depending on personalities, people respond differently to harm. Another example is the reward system. Reward dependence has been linked with the oxytocin system, with increased concentration of plasma oxytocin being observed, as well as increased volume in oxytocin-related regions of the hypothalamus.

A good example of personality linked to areas of the brain is a person who is more persistent that another would have more highly developed areas of the brain for persistence. Persistence has been associated with increased striatal-medial prefrontal cortex (MPFC) connectivity, increased activation of ventral striatal-orbitofrontal-anterior cingulate circuits, and increased salivary amylase levels indicative of increased noradrenergic tone.

The brain has plasticity and is malleable to external influences such as environmental factors.

There is significant evidence to show that environment influences personality. Life experiences predict personality differences. Studies have shown that experiences at home predict the development of personalities. This all begins with how a mother interacts with her baby. It was found in one study that children who were secure with their mothers were more confident and outgoing. Those who felt ambivalence showed signs of anxiety and anger.

COMPATIBILITY

Learning how personalities develop is helpful for understanding how people in the inner circle of one's relationships develop. But why do people become close to each other?

Similar interests and personality traits bring people together. Personality traits are probably most important. We don't limit compatibility with others to intimate relationships; we also include friends, family, acquaintances, and all those in the inner circle.

The definition of personality trait is characteristics of a person and imparts how one tends to think, feel, and behave on an ongoing basis. They persist in behavioral and emotional patterns. Isolated events do not determine personality. For example, a person can be angry, but that is not a personality trait unless anger is a persistent behavior, which then becomes a negative personality trait.

There are positive and negative personality traits.[12]

Positive Personality Traits

- open-minded and responsible
- flexible and adaptable
- ambitious and determined
- compassionate and empathetic
- patient
- confident and courageous
- critical and intelligent
- loyal
- creative and imaginative
- honest and fair
- helpful and generous

---

[12] Kail, Robert; Barnfield, Anne (2014). *Children and Their Development*. Pearson. ISBN 978-0-205-99302-4.

Negative Personality Traits

- dishonest and irresponsible
- disrespectful
- arrogant
- unmotivated and lazy
- inflexible and adamant
- manipulative
- uncompassionate
- critical and self-centered
- judgmental
- conceited and grandiose
- greedy

No one is perfect, and there is always a mix of positive and negative traits. One must weigh the good and the bad and determine their tolerance of any negative traits.

Other factors are also involved with relationship compatibility. With compatible relationships, people are similar in key characteristics and personality traits. This makes it possible to move through life at the same speed as their interests.

In compatible relationships, people have mutual, connected, or symbiotic goals. People work toward the same general objectives, whether obvious or obtuse. There is a reliance on each other. Individual goals may be separate, but there are also common goals for the relationship.

OUTER CIRCLE OF ACCEPTING OTHERS

Acceptance of others outside of one's inner circle means accepting people of different races, cultures, sexual orientations, genders, religious groups, political views, values, and so forth.

This form of acceptance embraces cognitive diversity. This means learning to tolerate and possibly even like people who think, act, and feel very differently from you. It means being free of bias and prejudice.

DIVERSITY

Accepting diversity is fundamental to our being. Diversity is a utilitarian since it makes the world a much more fascinating, enjoyable, and peaceful place. Diversity is a major creation by God. Mixing with those who are different from us means we get a sense of connection with them. For example, traveling in countries with different languages is more meaningful if one learns a few words or sentences in the language. The attempt means you care about them, and that creates a positive learning experience. We learn more about the world and ourselves in the process, which helps us grow intellectually and spiritually.

Acceptance of diversity can be difficult for those who are born into an isolated, homogeneous environment. Also, if parents and family are judgmental, biased, and prejudiced, learning about diversity is limited. Furthermore, each of us is raised differently, which adds to either acceptance or nonacceptance of diversity.

Early exposure to people of different races, cultures, and personalities allows for acceptance of others. Education, travel, and accepting parents allow for acceptance of others with diversity. For example, I grew up in an isolated, all-white, conservative farming community in Pennsylvania. My parents were involved in the Fresh Air Children's Program. Poor children of all races and cultures would come to the farm for a few weeks during the summer. I was exposed to Black, Asian, and Puerto Rican kids my age as a child. Some of these children have maintained relationships with our family into adulthood.

Do we have a moral responsibility or obligation to accept others?

THE MORALITY OF ACCEPTING OTHERS

The aptitude for acceptance as a natural pursuit of accepting others seems self-evident. Accepting others gives us a sense of worthiness and self-esteem. However accepting misery and social evil is not exclusionary simply by its existence. Miserable people and social evils are part of the natural inclusion of humans. This is not to be accepted, and when it affects individuals, one positive choice is to be strong. Weakness only produces more unhappiness. Being strong and functioning on the side of good will eventually overcome social evils. Nevertheless, the contrast should not prevent us from striving to improve our own—and other people's—conditions in life.

MORAL UTILITY AND RESPECT

Accepting others is a responsibility of utilitarianism. Utilitarianism is considered under consequentialist ethical theories that promote actions that maximize happiness and well-being for the majority of a population. Accepting others causes well-being for the community and the population as a whole. The basis is utility, which in terms of well-being, protection, goodness, and advancement must also come in defense of pain, evil, hatred, and unhappiness. Utilitarianism views all human beings as equal.

Jeremy Bentham and John Stuart Mill originated and developed the moral theory of utilitarianism, and much of their writing centered on pleasure and happiness as the moral end of humankind. However, utilitarianism considers more than pleasure.

The natural utility of humans is acceptance of diversity because diversity is our Creator's creation. The universal utilitarian criterion is the acceptance of other races, cultures, and behaviors that are not harmful to each other. This disallows hatred and prejudice.

Acceptance does not imply submission to all things good or bad. One can have no liking for a trait or behavior in an individual, group, or culture and remain with overall acceptance. For example, one may not like a culture that is manipulative or assertive, but that does not cause hatred, hostility, or prejudice.

There must be a distinction between acceptance and unacceptance. An individual or group that projects bad, hostile, nefarious actions or activities toward others should not be considered acceptable.

One can disagree with or object to others in terms of their opinions, behaviors, or values, but that must not create bias or hatred. There is allowance for acceptance of the individual or group under these conditions. The line is crossed when people cause harm to others. There is no utility in causing harm to others. That becomes the opposite to utilitarianism, which is called nefariousness, the badness toward the greatest number of people. Intolerant pressures, totalitarianism, and dictatorial instigations of opinion and values on others should be considered unacceptable.

Displaying hatred toward gays, Blacks, Asians, and so forth should be considered unacceptable; none of these people are doing anything to harm others. Only when an individual or group does harm to others must that be considered bad. However, the whole group should not receive hatred for single incidents.

Instilling religious values and values to the masses through government or education is not considered utilitarian, and it should not be accepted. Some Christian values create hostility and hatred toward others. Some state governments want to eliminate education of racial and social injustices that have historically occurred in the United States with the argument that Johnny and Mary may feel bad, but that is really just adults injecting their feelings into the equation. It is utilitarian for children to learn about past injustices so that the injustices are not repeated. There is a moral obligation for children and adults to learn about the Holocaust, genocides, slavery, and so forth. The Bible teaches about slavery of the Israelites in Egypt and their freedom. The book of Job is another example of bad things.

Respect and tolerance are virtues of utilitarianism. Respect is a positive feeling or action toward someone or something considered important or held in high esteem or regard. Respect conveys the highest regard for acceptance and tolerance. It morally presents itself as caring, concern, and empathy. Respect is different from tolerance, and it is a two-way street. One earns respect from another, and the other person must equally produce respect.

Different cultures have their own languages and ways of showing respect. In Islam, respect is shown by kissing the hands of parents, grandparents, and teachers. Japanese people bow as a greeting, and Chinese people bow to their elders.

Respect is considered a moral value in most cultures. Moral values influence participation in society. It helps individuals develop, improve, participate, and integrate into societies and cultures. Teaching the value of respect in childhood creates acceptance and tolerance. Respect is especially important in childhood since it serves as a basis of how children must conduct themselves in society.

Indigenous North Americans are an excellent example of moral and respectful values. Respect begins with the universe and nature and carries over into their community. In the universe and nature, they respect "Father Sky" and "Mother Earth." This parental example of the universe is handed down to children and reflected in the community.

SOCIAL CHOICE THEORY

Social choice theory is the theoretical framework for analysis of combining individual opinions, preferences, interests, or welfares to reach a collective decision or social welfare. Pleasure in this context means happiness or enjoyment. Welfare means health, happiness, and well-being. Preference is a technical term that is usually used to choose between alternatives. Preferences are central to decision theory because of this relation to behavior. It has to do with comparisons.

Social choice theory means projecting individual pleasure onto a group. Enacting a law that prevents harm to any individual in society is a social choice that provides well-being to all. Not enacting strict gun control does not fit into social choice theory. Individuals with guns can cause harm to others in society. Gun control lacks collective decision-making because a few are preventing collective decisions.

MORAL RELATIVISM

Metaethics is the attempt to understand the metaphysical, epistemological, semantic, and psychological, presuppositions, and commitments of moral thought, talk, and practice. This is divided into three types.

Moral nihilism, also known as ethical nihilism, is the metaethical view that nothing has intrinsic moral value. For example, a moral nihilist would say that killing someone, for whatever reason, is intrinsically neither morally right nor morally wrong.

Emotivism, in metaethics is the view that moral judgments do not function as statements of fact but rather as expressions of the speaker's or writer's feelings.

Metaethical relativism holds that moral judgments are not true or false in any absolute sense; they are only relative to particular standpoints. This idea is essential to just about any version of moral relativism. Some metaethical relativists focus more on the justification of moral judgments than on their truth.

Of the three subtypes, moral nihilism could be addressed with nefariousness; however, moral nihilism provides more of an explanation rather than the fact that immorality exists.

Nefariousness is a negative philosophical and ethical study. It could be studied scientifically. We know from functional magnetic resonance imaging studies that psychopaths have a dysfunctional prefrontal and frontal cortex. More studies of the brain could help us understand evil in humans.

Truth-value is defined as the attribute assigned to a proposition in respect to its truth or falsehood, which in classical logic has only two possible values (true or false).

AN INTRODUCTION TO MORAL RELATIVISM

Moral relativism is the idea that there is no universal or absolute set of moral principles. It's a version of morality that advocates "to each her own," and those who follow it say, "Who am I to judge?"

Defined by Wikipedia, moral relativism is used to describe several philosophical positions concerned with the differences in moral judgments across different peoples and their own particular cultures.

Modern ethical relativism has been divided into descriptive, metaethical, and normative moral relativism.

Descriptive moral relativism holds only that people disagree fundamentally about what is moral—with no judgment being expressed on the desirability of this. Descriptive moral relativism is a position that fundamental disagreements about the right course of action even when the same facts hold true and the same consequences seem likely to arise. It is the observation that different cultures have different moral standards. It does not necessarily advocate the tolerance of all behavior. Examples of descriptive moral relativism are how some cultures see homosexuality as immoral—and others do not. Some cultures think that polygamy is morally acceptable and should even be encouraged—while others see monogamy as the moral ideal. Some cultures practice slavery—while others find slavery morally abhorrent.

Metaethical moral relativism states that there are no objective grounds for preferring the moral values of one culture over another. Societies make their moral choices based on their unique beliefs, customs, and practices. Metaethical moral relativism holds that nobody is objectively right or wrong in such disagreements.

In metaethical moral relativism, people disagree about moral issues, and terms such as "good," "bad," "right," and "wrong" are not stand subject to universal principles. Instead, moral issues are relative to the traditions, convictions, or practices of an individual or a group of people. In other words, the Maasai tribe in Africa, the indigenous people of North America, and the Russians have their own moral values and ethical norms. The moral values are learned in each culture or group. Each culture understands that there are no higher moral values other than their own. As a result, there is no judgment of other cultures as to what is right or wrong.

Metaethical relativism is unacceptable to moral universalism, which argues that there are higher moral values that exist throughout all cultures and societies.

Normative moral relativism is the idea that all societies should accept each other's differing moral values, given that there are no universal moral principles. For example, just because prostitution is accepted in some cultures doesn't mean that other cultures cannot rightfully condemn it. Normative moral relativism holds that because nobody is right or wrong, everyone ought to tolerate the behavior of others even when considerably large disagreements about the morality of particular things exist.

Normative moral relativism does not agree with metaethical thesis, and it has normative implications on what we ought to do right or wrong. Normative moral relativism implies tolerance to behavior of others even when it runs counter to our personal or cultural moral standards. Moral normative relativism accepts all behaviors—morally—which means that individuals, cultures, and societies that cause hardship and suffering should not have tolerance accepted. This includes the same kinds of bad behavior in our society. It is perfectly reasonable and practical for a person or group to defend their subjective values against others—even if there is no universal prescription or morality.

We argue that universal principles should exist in all cultures and societies.

TOLERANCE IN MORAL RELATIVISM

Relativism can be considered, under normative morality, only on how people ought to behave toward those with whom they morally disagree. The most prominent normative position in this connection concerns tolerance. In recent years, the idea that we should be tolerant has been increasingly prominent, especially in regard to moral relativism. This means there should be policies that prevent interference with moral judgments we reject when the disagreement cannot be rationally resolved.

In all forms of moral relativism, tolerance is the only objective moral truth; all others are relative. Regardless of moral truth-values, moral standards, and behaviors between cultures and societies, tolerance is an objective value in and of itself. That could mean that tolerance could be accepted in some cultures and false in others. We would argue that tolerance is considered a moral good or truth, and it is good for all cultures and societies. If one disagrees with the moral values of one culture, under moral relativism, the judgment is relative and not absolute, which allows for tolerance.

TOLERANCE

Tolerance has many definitions that apply to physical sciences, engineering, and so forth, but we are defining tolerance here in terms of social acceptance. The definition of tolerance is a fair and objective attitude toward others, and it is usually a conscious effort from an individual. Tolerance allows one to encounter and endure someone or something that is different or contentious without voicing negative opinions. It means being free from the judgments of others.

Tolerance is a utilitarian principle. Studies have shown that people who live in a tolerant society are more likely to experience happiness. Does tolerance cause a happy society—or does a happy society produce tolerance? It really does not matter because there is tolerance in both situations. It promotes individualism. It allows self-expression, self-esteem, and knowledge. These features of self-autonomy lead to personal happiness. Tolerance is accommodating the differences of others and being empathetic to the individual's beliefs, culture, and unique behaviors.

We all encounter others who are annoying, have different

opinions, and have different behaviors. Understanding their issues through communication creates tolerance.

Tolerance is a cognitive function of the brain. It is not totally intrinsic; it is learned. An example is found in social media. Research has shown that using social media makes an individual more tolerant. In some situations, it is found to be up to 80 percent more tolerant. This is explained by exposing the brain to the various views of others more frequently, which makes it easier to revisit new ideas and learn tolerance. The more exposure a person has to new information, the more accepting they will become to that new information. The brain is more likely to accept repetitive information that it is exposed to over time. This will create a more tolerant person.

Tolerance is also present on a larger scale. We recognize religious, political, and cultural tolerance. In a free society, tolerance is essential. Otherwise, society would be chaotic. Tolerance provides a more stable, cohesive, orderly, and peaceful society. People who are free to express themselves without fear of persecution are more likely to live happier lives as functional members of society. A group, society, or country that is intolerant, forcing their population to conform to one social mold, leads to unhappiness and rebellion.

The utility of tolerance is in preventing violence. Race-based and religious-based violence are reduced in a tolerant society. A society without violence is a moral society, sharing respect and empathy for others. A happy society is strong, energetic, and productive.

Tolerance can take a long time to develop in a society. It took nearly sixty years in the twentieth century for a black man to be allowed to play Major League Baseball and professional football.

MORAL JUDGMENT

Moral judgment refers to a decision about what one should do in a morally problematic situation and what is right and what is wrong when deciding what to do.

Judgments involve our intuitions or critical analysis based

on reality and our capacity to reach decisions through reasoning. Intuition is the ability to understand something immediately without conscious reasoning.

Moral judgments refer to judgments that have moral content; they are used to evaluate situations, individual and society behaviors, societal norms, courses of action, and so forth. Unfortunately, when intuition is used for moral judgment, conscious reasoning has no role in the judgments. The emotions and feelings can create an irrational, unethical, or chaotic outcome.

Supporters of the intuitive emotional theory—the theory of sentiment—for moral judgment use an argument concerning psychopaths. They state that psychopaths are intelligent, but they lack empathy, grief, sympathy, and so forth. Therefore, since they lack emotions, they also lack moral judgment. However, this is incorrect reasoning since psychopaths lack executive function of the brain, which does not allow for moral judgment and knowing right from wrong.

An argument that is more rational is that of deontology by Immanuel Kant, a German philosopher. Deontological ethics holds that some acts are morally obligatory regardless of their consequences for human welfare. Descriptive of such ethics are such expressions as "Duty for duty's sake," "Virtue is its own reward," and "Let justice be done." Deontology is an ethical theory that uses rules to distinguish right from wrong.

Kant believed that ethical actions follow universal moral laws. Kant puts rationality at the center of morality and moral judgment. He proposed that morality is derived from reason and that moral requirements are based on a standard of rationality.

Moral judgment switched from philosophy to psychology in the twentieth century; however, moral judgment remains a philosophical issue. Lawrence Kohlberg, in 1984, originated the psychological theory of the development of moral judgments. Kohlberg's six stages of moral development have been grouped into three levels: pre-conventional, conventional, and post-conventional. He patterned the six stages of moral development in children after Jean Piaget's famous cognitive-development theory:

Stage 1: obedience and punishment
Stage 2: self-interest
Stage 3: interpersonal accord and conformity
Stage 4: authority and maintaining social order
Stage 5: social contract
Stage 6: universal ethical principles

LEVEL 1: PRE-CONVENTIONAL MORALITY

Pre-conventional morality is the first level of childhood moral development, and it lasts until approximately age nine. At this stage, morality is learned from adults in their specific culture. The child learns that which is good or bad according to consequences.

Level 1 includes stages 1 and 2. Stage 1 is child obedience and punishment and orientation to moral principles. The incentive for the child is being good in order to prevent punishment.

Stage 2 is individualism and exchange. In this stage, the child recognizes there is not just one right view that is taught; there may be variations or other right views. They learn that individuals have different views.

LEVEL 2: CONVENTIONAL MORALITY

Stages 3 and 4 are present in level 2. Level 2 is characterized by an acceptance of social rules concerning right and wrong. The conventional level includes adolescents and young adults who internalize the moral standards of valued adult role models. Also, reasoning is based on the norms of the group to which the person belongs. The conventional level is important in terms of its social system. The system stresses the responsibilities of moral relationships.

Social order is seen as desirable and must, therefore, influence the view of what is right and wrong.

Stage 3 is good interpersonal relationships in which the individual is viewed by others as a good person.

Stage 4 is maintaining the social order by the individual. At this stage, the individual becomes aware of the rules of their culture of society. Also, judgments concern observing the rules and upholding laws to avoid punishment and guilt.

LEVEL 3—POST-CONVENTIONAL MORALITY

This third level or moral development includes stages 5 and 6. It is characterized by an individual's understanding of universal ethical principles, which are considered abstract and ill-defined. Such principles include preservation of life, respect, honest, and dignity. Individual judgment is based on self-chosen principles, and moral reasoning is based on individual rights and justice.

According to Kohlberg, this level of moral reasoning is only achieved in 10–15 percent of capable individuals. This means that about 85 percent accept their moral views from others.

Stage 5 is social contract and individual rights. The individual becomes aware that rules and laws exist for the good of the majority, but there are situations where the laws and rules can work against the interests of particular individuals.

Stage 6 is universal principles. Individuals at this stage have developed their own moral values that may or may not fit into their culture or society. This will involve human rights, justice, and equality, which society may not observe in total. The individual will defend these principles—even at the expense of their own consequences in a society that may be against them.

Although the moral development theory provides how morality develops in children and individuals, the theory offers no moral problem-solving. How does moral judgment solve moral problems? It incorporates reason, logic, experience, facts, knowledge, and so forth to reach a solution or moral standard. However, recent psychology research argues that intuition and feelings in individuals make moral judgments.

An example that is frequently quoted for moral judgment is people advocating for or against the death penalty. A person with a vested interest in ending the death penalty does so not just because they believe it is the right thing to do (killing is wrong) but because it is the best thing to do (the death penalty does not deter crime).

We discussed moral judgment in moral relativism, but moral judgment is also present in moral absolutism and moral universalism.

Moral absolutism is an ethical view that all actions are intrinsically right or wrong. An example of moral absolutism is stealing. Stealing might be considered to be always immoral—even if done for the well-being of others (stealing food to feed a starving family) or if it does promote good in the end. The moral judgment could also apply to murder or bribery.

Moral absolutism is in conflict with other normative ethics, such as consequentialism and moral universalism.

Consequentialism judges whether or not something is right by the outcome or consequences. For instance, most people would agree that lying is wrong. However, if telling a lie would help save a person's life, consequentialism says the lie would be considered morally right. Also, moral absolutism is not the same as moral universalism.

Universalism holds merely that what is right or wrong is independent of custom or opinion as opposed to moral relativism, but not necessarily that what is right or wrong is independent of context or consequences as in absolutism. Moral universalism is compatible with moral absolutism, but it also positions such as consequentialism.

Moral universalism can also be explained as a system of ethics that applies to all people—regardless of race, color, nationality, religion, or culture—and must have moral plurality among individuals, customs, societies, and nations in which morality asserts universal principles, moral values, and authority. Universal principles include honesty, dignity, respect, rights, and equality. A moral value is a universally accepted principle that governs day-to-day living. These principles are important in maintaining unity, harmony, and honor between people.

The earliest form of moral universalism can be found in the Seven Laws of Noah (Hebrew: נח בני מצוות שבע, Sheva Mitzvot B'nei Noach). They originated from descendants of Noah who were commanded with seven precepts: to establish laws, which included blasphemy, idolatry, adultery, bloodshed, theft, and eating the blood of a living animal. These seven laws can be considered universal principles.

Immanuel Kant wrote about moral universalism and could also be considered an early writer of utilitarianism. In moral universalism, the shared moral and ethical characteristics of humanity emphasize the principles of justice, fairness, and equality. It provides a normative perspective on humanity.

The most common example of moral universalism is equality in the workplace regardless of gender. Other examples are Black, Brown, and Asian people as presidents or CEOs and equality in the workplace. This is the most common example of moral universalism. It provides one small part of humanity where moral universalism is applied, but what about cultures and societies as a whole?

Moral universalism is difficult to practice in most societies. Buddhism is one example. Many Christians have difficulties with moral universalism. Prejudices, equality, hypocrisy, fears, and so forth obstruct universalism.

The Abrahamic religions (Islam, Judaism, and Christianity) follow moral absolutism, even though universal principles were initially established. Absolutism is the theory that some actions are good or evil regardless of the context. Absolutism creates problems in humanity that universalism avoids. As an example, the different principles between Catholics and Protestants caused the Thirty-Year War in Europe in the 1600s.

Most religions subscribe to moral absolutism, especially Christianity. Christians adhere to moral absolutist positions since their moral system is derived from divine commandments. Therefore, such a moral system is absolute and usually considered perfect and unchanging, especially in their strict judgmental structure. They assert that the absolute laws of morality are inherent in the nature of people. For example, someone who absolutely believes in nonviolence considers it wrong to use violence—even in self-defense.

SUMMARY

This chapter addresses acceptance of other people. We divided this type of acceptance between one's inner circle and outer circle of people. The inner circle is made up of family, friends, and loved ones, which has a different psychological impact, such as personality traits. The outer circle is more complex psychologically, philosophically, and socially. This form of acceptance involves ethics and morality. We did a detailed analysis of the morality of accepting others. Anyone wanting to make changes in their acceptance of others should learn about the morality of acceptance, including tolerance and respect.

CHAPTER 7
EXTREME REJECTION; HATE

The most extreme and nefarious form of
rejection of others is hate or hatred.

Many notable figures throughout history have spoken out against hatred and hate crimes. Here are seven quotes from well known personalities, ranging from the most ancient of religions, Buddhism, to John Lennon, which encourage us to put an end to hate crime.

Hatred does not cease by hatred, but only
by love; this is the eternal rule.
—Siddhārtha Gautama, *The Dhammapada:
The Sayings of the Buddha*

In the practice of tolerance, one's enemy is the best teacher.
—The Dalai Lama

No one is born hating another person because of the color of his skin, or his background, or his religion. People must learn to hate, and if they can learn to hate, they can be taught to love, for love comes more naturally to the human heart than its opposite.
—Nelson Mandela

Misunderstanding arising from ignorance breeds fear,
and fear remains the greatest enemy of peace.
—Lester B. Pearson

> Why is it that, as a culture, we are more comfortable seeing two men holding guns than holding hands?
> —Ernest Gaines

> You cannot hate other people without hating yourself.
> —Oprah Winfrey

> Don't hate what you don't understand.
> —John Lennon

We separated hate from all the other chapters because hate can be personal, social, or societal. It expresses a wide range of feelings. You might hear someone say they hate spinach or the President. We are usually able to discern as a society those insignificant hates from those that are worrisome. However, those that are worrisome need improvement for managing these severe hates. We also separated this chapter from the rest because of the severe emotions and behaviors of hatred.

This chapter describes the different types of hate. Much of the chapter is an attempt to explain the psychology and brain function associated with hate. We also address the psychological transition from hate to violence. Hate speech and hate crimes are also addressed.

Hate is defined as a feeling of intense fear and anger with a dislike toward certain people, ideas, or objects.

Wikipedia defines hatred as a very angry emotional response toward certain people or ideas, usually related to disliking someone or something. Hatred is often associated with intense feelings of anger, contempt, and disgust.

Hatred is an intense negative emotional response toward certain people, things, or ideas, usually related to opposition or revulsion toward something. Hatred is often associated with intense feelings of anger, contempt, and disgust. Hatred is sometimes seen as the opposite of love.

Hate involves an appraisal that a person or group is evil.

In the definitions of hatred, one of the key words is angry

emotion. Hate anger as an emotion can be expressed with very little expression and intensity, such as a child saying he or she hates vegetables, but hatred is mostly thought of as a more long-standing and more intense type of anger held within.

Hate, like love, takes different shapes and forms in different languages. There are different meanings in English, French (*haine*), and German (*Hass*), which depend on how it is used in a sentence.

Hatred is learned emotion that arises out of abuse and manipulation by parents who are expressing hatred. Also, hatred is the deep psychological response to feeling trapped or being unable to understand certain sociological phenomena.

Aristotle viewed hatred as distinct from anger and rage, describing hate as a desire to annihilate an object.

In certain cases, religions can regard other religions as evil, which on certain occasions can be true and acutely felt.

NORMATIVE HATRED

Normative hatred results when hated moral values and truths are violated by an individual or group in society. Although lying appears to have become a norm in the twenty-first century, most of society agrees that lying is wrong. When someone tells a lie, we feel contempt and find them to be targets of normative hate. Honesty is considered a universal principle, which can take on absolutism in the form of hatred. Threatening societal rules, loss of choices, and loss of rights can lead to normative hatred.

IDEOLOGICAL HATRED

Ideological hatred occurs when a political policy is not observed or does not provide significant differences of opinion in a society. Examples include when ethnic or cultural homogeny is at risk from foreigners with immigration, jobs, or economics. The hatred is a result of fear and irrational thinking. The individuals in the homogeneous group reinforce each other's irrational fears and reinforce hatred.

RETRIBUTIVE HATRED

Retributive hatred occurs when someone causes harm to an individual or group. The feelings resulting from harmful action by others are anger, indignation, resentment, and a desire for revenge. These feelings can lead to hatred. An example is a person killing a son or daughter in a school shooting. Hate may be directed toward the killer and school for not protecting the child. These feelings are normal, and forgiveness may be considered abnormal.

MALICIOUS HATRED

Malicious hatred results from an individual or group hating another for their goodness or successes. It is a jealous hate. We see this when a student receives all A's, and their classmates hate them for it.

BRAIN FUNCTION AND THE PSYCHOLOGY OF HATRED

What parts of the brain are responsible for hatred and anger? This has been investigated using a functional MRI. This technology is a special MRI in which the part of the brain "lights up" (with increased activity) when a person is asked specific questions or scenarios. In this specific hate experiment, people had their brains scanned while viewing pictures of people they hated. The results showed increased activity in the middle frontal gyrus, right putamen, bilaterally in the premotor cortex, in the frontal pole, and bilaterally in the medial insular cortex of the human brain.

Selective sound sensitivity syndrome or misophonia is a condition that causes a person to become angry when certain sounds trigger the condition.

THE PSYCHOLOGY OF HATE

Psychologically, hatred involves anger, fear, paranoia, and phobias.

Anger is an intense negative emotion that is usually present in hate, but the cause is often an intense form of fear, such as paranoia or a phobia. Fear can lead to anger and turn to hatred.

ANGER

Anger is an intense emotional state involving a strong uncomfortable and noncooperative response to a perceived provocation, hurt, or threat. It may also be called wrath, like the wrath of God, or rage. Anger is especially incorporated into normative and ideological hatred.

Anger can be expressed as a mild to severe emotion. At all levels, anger can be expressed toward oneself or another. One could be angry from tripping over something and falling or at another person for causing the fall. It could be expressed from raising one's voice to screaming. Mild anger does not cause much of a physiological response, but the physical signs are obvious, such as lowering the eyebrows or squinting. Mild anger can be considered as an annoyance. Moderate anger could lead to aggression, but severe anger is expressed in the form of rage and physical harm toward others.

The physiology of moderate to severe anger is similar to that of fear. Adrenaline (epinephrine) and norepinephrine are released to cause increased heart rate, blood pressure, and breathing. It is similar to the fight-or-flight response of fear.

Anger, when viewed as a protective response or instinct to a perceived threat, is considered positive. The negative expression of this state is known as aggression. Acting on this misplaced state is rage due to possible potential errors in perception or judgment.

Anger causes a reduction in cognitive ability. Perception is inaccurate, and external stimuli have indiscriminate perception. Real danger seems less risky, and there is more risk in making decisions. In terms of intergroup relationships, anger makes people think in more negative and prejudiced terms about outsiders.

In ideological hatred, anger makes people less trusting and slower to attribute good qualities to outsiders. When a political or ideological group is in conflict with a rival group, the politically or ideologically inferior group will feel more anger.

We have discussed anger and how it is incorporated into the definitions of hate and hatred, but there is a significant difference between hate and anger in terms of emotions.

The main difference between anger and hate is that though both are negative emotions that all humans feel at times, anger does not last long—but the hate usually persists for a longer time. Anger is like having the flu, and hate is like having cancer. Anger may have a distortion of perception, but hate has a significant distortion of anger and fear. Hate shuts down reason and embraces a mild form of repressed rage. Anger may make it difficult to think, but with hate, there is no ability to reason or think rationally. Delusional thinking may be involved with hate.

Hate is very destructive to others and to the self. It leads to solitary isolation or with a group that suffers from similar hate ideation.

There are differences in the causes of anger and hate. The cause of anger is superficial, due to an irritational or bad situation. The cause for hate is deep-rooted and has been continuing for a longer time. The intensity of anger is comparatively low, but it can climb to the level of rage. Hate is deeper and more intense.

Anger has a relatively low impact on others in comparison to hate. Hate causes the person to develop intense emotions like revenge and disgust. Eventually, they will be compelled to take intense and extreme reactions such as physical injury and damage. This is another major difference between the two.

Goodness, empathy, and forgiveness can develop from anger.

Nothing good can come from hate because hate takes possession of the hater. If you hate someone or something, you have placed what you hate beyond compassion and understanding. The hated person becomes an object.

FEAR

Anger is a part of hate, but the main cause of hatred is fear. This can be fear of others or fears that we have within ourselves and project on others. A person can immediately and unconsciously turn fear into anger because fear leaves us feeling vulnerable, and anger gives us a sense of power. Humans value power over vulnerability because power makes us feel safer. When fear turns to anger, the next step is to despise, and this can also turn to hate. This leads to a fear-anger-hatred cycle.

People frequently consult their group to reinforce their fears, and they form aggression toward the outside individual or group that is different and feared. People have their own belief fears, and when they identify these fearful beliefs in others, their fear is projected to the other in the form of hatred. Sometimes people project their badness toward others to protect their goodness. The badness can be in the form of hatred.

Fear, anger, and hatred became prominent to everyone via the internet and social media.

PARANOIA

Paranoia is a mental condition characterized by delusions of persecution, unwarranted jealousy, or exaggerated executions of the self or others, and it is typically elaborated into an organized system.

Paranoia is defined by Wikipedia as an instinct or thought process that is believed to be heavily influenced by anxiety or fear, often to the point of delusion and irrationality.

Vigilance is defined as the action of keeping watch for possible danger or difficulty.

Hypervigilance is defined as the elevated state of constantly assessing potential threats around you—and it is often the result of trauma. People who have been in combat, have survived abuse, or have posttraumatic stress disorder (PTSD) can exhibit hypervigilance.

Paranoid cognition is explained when individuals are self-conscious or feel under evaluative scrutiny, they tend to overestimate the extent to which they are the target of others' attention. As a result, they make overly personalistic attributions about others' behaviors.

Paranoid thinking can include persecutory beliefs or conspiracies concerning a perceived threat toward themselves or their group. They think, *Everyone is out to get me.*

Phobias are totally separate from paranoia due to the severity of fear in phobias and the extreme irrationality of paranoia.

False accusations, general mistrust, and making threats toward other people or groups frequently accompany paranoia. Paranoia is a central theme of psychosis, and all thoughts and emotional processes have lost touch with reality.

Paranoia can develop during childhood development, as a result of social situations, in mental health disorders, from certain neurological conditions, and as a result of recreational drugs or drug abuse.

Paranoia can develop during childhood from untrusting parental relationships. These environments could include parents being very disciplinary, stringent, or unstable. On the other hand, overprotection and indulging the child can make them suspicious of others. Experiences likely to enhance or manifest the symptoms of paranoia include increased rates of disappointment, stress, and hopelessness.

Social experiences can cause paranoia. Certain risk factors increase the likelihood of developing paranoia:

- confusing or unexplainable situations
- low self-esteem

- worry and anxiety
- restricted, rigid, and narrow-minded thinking
- insecurity
- isolation, urban living, and extreme environmental living
- past trauma
- feeling negative about oneself

Life experiences that contribute to paranoia involve fear, vulnerability, stress, isolation, and dangerous situations.

Media that expresses violence, crime, or terrorism can cause feelings of paranoia.

Paranoia can be found in many psychological disorders, including delusional disorder, paranoid personality disorder, paranoid schizophrenia, paranoid depression, and dementia.

Paranoia is found in neurological diseases, such as Huntington's disease, Parkinson's disease, strokes, Alzheimer's disease, and other forms of dementia. Severe insomnia without sleep can lead to paranoia and hallucinations. Studies have shown that loss of hearing for an extended period of time can lead to paranoia.

Recreational drugs—including cocaine, cannabis, ecstasy, LSD, and amphetamines–can cause paranoia. People are more prone to paranoia when they have underlying anxiety, phobias, or stresses. Abuse of alcohol can lead to Wernicke's syndrome, which causes paranoia.

DIAGNOSIS OF PARANOIA

Persons with paranoia have a distortion-biased reality caused by a person or thing. They exhibit hostile, dishonest beliefs. Symptoms can be mild, and a paranoid individual may view an incidental, unintentional action by another person as intentionally directed toward them. Extreme symptoms include violence.

Paranoid persons have feelings of powerless, depression, and isolation. Relinquishing activities are characteristics that could be associated with those exhibiting more frequent paranoia.

Persecutory delusions and false beliefs create thoughts of being harassed, threatened, harmed, subjugated, persecuted, accused, mistreated, wronged, tormented, disparaged, or vilified by individuals or groups.

PARANOIA AND VIOLENCE

Individuals with paranoid delusions will take actions based on their beliefs. If they have delusions of violence, they tend to become violent. Studies have shown that violent behaviors are more common in certain types of paranoid individuals, mainly those considered to have persecution paranoia.

Researchers have found associations between childhood abusive behaviors and the violent behaviors in paranoid psychotic individuals. This could be a result of their inability to cope with aggression and other people, especially when constantly attending to potential threats.

PHOBIA

A phobia is a form of anxiety defined by a persistent and excessive fear of an object, person, or situation. When defined as persistent, that means more than six months of avoiding the situation. Symptoms may also include distress, fainting, panic attacks, and hatred. Specific phobias may be caused by a negative experience with a person, object, or situation in early childhood.

Social phobia is when a person fears a situation due to worries about others judging them. If the individual or group is from a different race or socioeconomic group, hatred can be present. An example is xenophobia. Xenophobia is the dislike, prejudice, or hatred toward or against people from other countries.

Fear is prevalent in mental health disorders, such as phobias and paranoia. Individuals with these disorders can be prone to hatred and violence.

HATRED AND VIOLENCE

A prerequisite to violent hatred is diminished or absent morality and the consequences of immorality. Religions, especially Christianity, are not necessarily equivalent to morality. A prime historical example is during the Thirty-Year religious War between the Catholics and Protestants, eight million Europeans died. Didn't the Bible say, "Thou shalt not kill"? Imagine the hatred and violence associated with that war!

Another prerequisite is fanaticism, which is a belief or behavior involving uncritical zeal or obsessive enthusiasm. This is a biased, uncritical, and blind adherence to an ideology. They lack empathy, guilt, and shame in their hatred toward others. These violent haters disengage from their actions and think that their actions are justified. They lack any feelings that they caused in the suffering of others.

Fanatics are usually isolated in like-minded groups. This crowd is also capable of violence because they all have a fanatical, extreme ideology. In fact, the whole group is isolated from reality. Their preexisting beliefs create their perceptions and intentions.

GROUP VIOLENCE

Individuals are more likely to do bad things in a group than as an individual. The group creates identity, creates camaraderie, and allows for security. The group fills a void in their insecurity and identity. This allows for a collective lack of conscience. The group has a permit to become a mob and sees freedom in violence.

The ideological group feels righteous and just in their behavior because they see others as illegitimate or evil. In these violent acts, the individuals are protected by the group by anonymity. In psychology, this is referred to as herd behavior. This is to be distinguished from herd immunity as it relates to immunity from infections after vaccinations or an infection.

Individuals who are at risk for hatred and violence are young boys and men who grew up unloved and in abusive environments, underachievers, and those who have behavioral and personality disorders. It is not known why some persons progress to violence, and others remain with hatred and no violence.

UNWANTED AND ABUSED CHILDREN

When a baby is delivered into the world, the first contact is the mother. Under normal environmental conditions, a bond forms between the baby and the mother. She is the caregiver who normally nurtures the baby. Immediate skin-to-skin contact at birth creates an immediate bond. The first months to a year are also critical for both parents to show love and affection for the baby.

When a baby does not develop a close bond with their mother, they may become detached. This results in a condition called attachment disorder. It usually happens to babies and children who have been neglected, abused, or removed from parents or caregivers.

Early signs of attachment disorder may be excessive crying or not crying at all. The baby may have abnormal sleep patterns and may not want to be touched or held. They may not interact or smile to adults, and they may not interact with adults. They may suck their thumbs past the age of five. They may play alone rather than with other children. The child may be aggressive to other children or adults. As they become older, they are more withdrawn, fearful, untrusting, and anxious. In school, they become underachievers. By the time they are teenagers, they have developed anxiety and depression. They also are likely to be in trouble with the police.

Children who are not raised in a loving, caring, safe, and respectful environment will likely grow up feeling untrusting, unsafe, and anxious. They tend to not trust themselves or others.

Another key component is rebellion against adults, authorities, and peers who are seen as part of the established norm. They seek those who are on the fringes of society. This provides opportunities for young boys to engage in extreme groups that weaponize their grievances and anger. Their rebellion finds a home in extremist groups. Young boys are more vulnerable, impulsive, and risky. It is easy to lure these boys into combat activities such as mixed martial arts. The next step is violence.

UNDERACHIEVERS

Underachievers have deep-rooted inferiority complexes and frustrations. Their frustration leads to blame and resentment, which leads to hatred. They compensate for their poor self-esteem by attaching to something they perceive as strong, like an extremist ideological group. The association with the group provides feelings of prestige, recognition, or glory. They hope the organization will rub off on them and compensate for what they could not achieve individually. All of the individuals in the group have not done well in life. The group rallies around a leader who appears strong and is good at articulating and promoting their hatred.

Political parties with extremist views are a good example. Donald Trump's campaign in 2016 targeted low-income white Americans without a college degree. He played into their hidden fears by vehemently attacking undocumented immigrants and Muslims. Trump was a voice for the members in the group who were reluctant to express their hatred for fear of the repercussions.

Underachievers have had some form of abuse in their past, usually as a child or teenager. They are associated with fighting and violence. As they become members of the group, violence is reinforced.

BEHAVIOR AND PERSONALITY DISORDERS

These individuals engage in violence outside the group, but they often use the group's ideology to justify their violence. These individuals are frequently referred to as a "lone wolf" with a "hero mentality."

These individuals are frequently referred to as conduct disorders or psychopaths.

Normal children can tell right from wrong by the age of five and no longer have the anger and defiance of the terrible twos. However, children with conduct disorders cannot tell right from wrong and start having very abnormal behavior that can be recognized between the ages of six and fifteen. Conduct disorder is an antisocial behavioral disorder. They have trouble following rules, and they struggle to show empathy. Typically their behavior includes aggression, such as starting fights. They destroy property with disregard for rules or laws. Chronic lying and dishonesty are part of their behavior. They engage in bullying and harm others. These behaviors give them substantial pleasure. They injure animals or pets by pulling their tails or throwing them. It can lead to the point of killing the pets. They lack any remorse or empathy for their behavior. Teenagers who have access to firearms may use them. In their teenage years, they may force someone into sexual activity or set fires. Approximately 25 percent of individuals with CD eventually arrive in prison.

The diagnosis is obscure because they are often thought of as a "bad kid," and they don't get seen by child psychologists. After eighteen, they are considered antisocial personality disorders or psychopaths. These young men are the serial killers at schools, grocery stores, synagogues, and so forth. They are isolated due to their behaviors and are easily influenced by hate groups.

HATRED IN RELIGION

The three ancient religions—Hinduism, Jainism, and Buddhism—do not support hatred, hate speech, or violence. It was only when the three Abrahamic religions evolved—Islam, Judaism, and Christianity—that hate, hate speech, and violence took place in humanity. What is the reasoning for this strong emotion? There was significant turmoil in Abraham's life, which caused hatred. This emotion was never resolved and persisted into the three religions.

There was also a power struggle with the Abrahamic religions, which persists to this day. Therefore, hatred is sanctioned by the Abrahamic religions.

Judaism, the religion in which Christianity gradually developed, had a Hebrew word describing the psalmist's "perfect hatred."

> Do not hate those who hate you, Lord, and abhor you and those who rise up against you? I have nothing but hatred for them; I count them my enemies. Search me, O God, and know my heart test me and know my anxious thoughts. See if there is any offensive way in me, and lead me the way everlasting. (Psalm 139:22 NIV)

This means that it brings a process to completion.

Islamic records explain how Islam developed around hatred, which is considered the source of evil and that adherents endeavored to spread the Qur'anic faith as the very means for the eradication of hatred and evil.

Hatred speech is also commonly found in religions. This is particularly found in Christians with extreme opinions about different races, ethnic groups, or gender identities. It also explains how religion aims to convert new followers and how extreme speech against other religions or their followers. This is an effective tool for changing others' beliefs.

It is contradictory to Jesus preaching on the Sermon on the Mount to love your enemies, but some Christians cannot accept others for who they are, resulting in hate speech.

THE LEGALITY OF HATE EXPRESSIONS

Hate speech and hate crimes can fall under the legal system. The two areas involve hate speech and hate crimes. There are no hate speech laws in the U.S. after several attempts to create laws or regulations.

It is highly debated and contested due to the First Amendment of the U.S. Constitution. However, but hate crime laws do exist in the United States.

Hate speech is defined as public speech that expresses hate and encourages violence toward a person or group based on something such as race, religion, sex, sexual orientation, ethnic group, nationality, or disability. Hate speech incorporates verbal anger and discrimination toward another individual or group. The most severe form of hate speech is directed toward violence. Legal definitions of hate speech vary from country to country.

There has been much debate over freedom of speech, hate speech, and hate speech legislation in most countries. Many countries in Europe have laws against individuals or groups that express hatred in the form of genocide. The penalties are several years in prison and large fines.

WORDS ARE POWERFUL, USE THEM RESPECTFULLY!

HATE SPEECH ON SOCIAL MEDIA AND THE INTERNET

Censorship is defined as the suppression or prohibition of any part of books, films, or news that is considered obscene, politically unacceptable, or a threat to security. In other words, the regulation imposes censorship on all media.

Censorship in the United States has been in almost all forms of media. The only complete censorship on the internet has been child pornography. Adult pornography is accessible on the internet, but what about hate speech?

With pressure from more than one hundred advocacy women's groups and Congress, in 2013, Facebook agreed to change their hate speech policies. Data released regarding content that promoted domestic and sexual violence against women led to the withdrawal of advertising by fifteen large companies.

At the urge of the European Union code of conduct, on May

31, 2016, Facebook, Twitter, Google, and Microsoft formed an agreement to remove illegal hate speech posted on their services within twenty-four hours.

The companies that have hate speech policies include Facebook and YouTube. How extensive are their policies if hate speech exists on both platforms? We certainly have no statistical data to know how much hate speech has been removed by these two companies versus the amount of hate speech that breaks through their policies and algorithms.

Cyber hate crimes have been added in many European countries. Since 2006, with the Additional Protocol to the Convention on Cybercrime, most members have committed to punish racist and xenophobic hate speech on the internet.

Censorship has been accepted by most media today except the internet and social media. There is much debate, and people like Donald Trump—who sent so much hate speech on Twitter and finally got removed—created more extensive debate. Elon Musk, the owner of Twitter, is making freedom of speech more controversial.

Free speech advocates, scholars, and activists have argued against any limitation of hate speech in America. Civil liberties activists agree that censoring hate speech may protect minorities and the vulnerable, but they argue that laws may also be used against them. This appears to be a weak argument.

Hate speech theory has also come under attack. Hate speech theories depend on when and who describes their theory. Proponents of freedom of hate speech date back to John Locke in 1689. In his "Letter Concerning Tolerance," he claimed that coercive matters of conscience can undercut the moral legitimacy of the oppressor's cause. In other words, one must be given the freedom to decide on hate speech; otherwise, the decision is not ethical. It is simply a matter of submission as a way of avoiding punishment.

John Stuart Mill wrote that public discourse ought to serve as a marketplace of ideas. He claimed that hate speech is an unavoidable part of the wider current of free speech. Mill thought there exists no partial truth; everything must be debated in order to determine what is true and what is false. This theory prizes the community's progression over individual desires.

John Stuart Mill said, "They [an individual] have no authority to decide the question for all mankind, and exclude every other person from the means of judging ... All silencing of discussion is an assumption of infallibility." He asserts the necessity of hate speech as a stepping stone to truth. Denying others the ability to evaluate statements because one believes those words to be offensive is making a unilateral decision that is ultimately harmful to the collective good.

Although these thinkers believe speech should be limited in certain contexts, they firmly contend that all speech, including hate speech, is a part of the growth and development of a community. It appears that Mill was contradicting himself. He was a big proponent of utilitarianism, which is the greatest good for the greatest number of people. How can hate speech, which is bad, be good for the greatest number of people?

The theory took a turn for more restriction due to World War II, the Holocaust, racial turmoil in America, and violence against Black people.

Case law has come before the U.S. Supreme Court in attempts to regulate hate speech. Each time, the Supreme Court has ruled in favor of freedom of speech and against regulations of hate speech. Hate speech theory has now been associated with liberals attempting to regulate hate speech.

The Heritage Foundation, a conservative think tank, has been critical of hate speech theory. They agree with Locke and Mill. They have argued that hate speech theory obliterates the ethical responsibility of the individual. They also argue that the theory assumes bad faith on the part of people regardless of their stated intentions.

Viewpoint discrimination has also been used as an argument against laws that regulate hate speech. Viewpoint discrimination is a concept in United States jurisprudence related to the First Amendment to the U.S. Constitution.

If a speech act is treated differently by a government entity based on the viewpoint it expresses, this is considered viewpoint discrimination. This basically states that it would be difficult to rule against what is considered hate speech versus another form of hate speech.

The First Amendment can address hate speech, but the U.S. Supreme Court keeps overlooking important designations. The U.S. Constitution was written on September 17, 1787, to bring the states, together under the U.S. Constitution. There was religious turmoil between the states, which caused the formation of the First Amendment. The founders were concerned about the connection of church and government in Europe, especially with all the religious wars. The First Amendment to the United States Constitution was not written until December 15, 1791:

> Congress shall make no law respecting an establishment of religion, or prohibiting the free exercise thereof; or abridging the freedom of speech, or of the press; or the right of the people peaceably to assemble, and to petition the Government for a redress of grievances.

Even though proponents of freedom of speech like to quote their "First Amendment rights," the First Amendment does not prevent censorship. The people who recite the First Amendment freely to insist the amendment gives them the right to say anything are misguided. The First Amendment has limitations. It does not allow for speech communication of serious threats of bodily injury or death to others, speech that incites imminent lawless action where that action is likely to occur, or conspire to commit criminal acts.

There is a solution to appeasing the First Amendment and lawfully restricting or regulating hate speech. Speech that would accommodate the First Amendment could be divided into hostility speech and hate speech. Hostility is unfriendliness or dislike toward opposition. Hostility speech fully allows for freedom of speech without any laws or restrictions. This is considered passive speech.

Hate is an extremely intense bad feeling toward someone. It is associated with action and violence. Hate speech could then be processed under laws or regulations. The First Amendment does not allow speech that leads to violence and harm of others. Using logic:

If A equals B and B equals C, then A equals C. If hate speech equals violence, and violence equals death, then hate speech equals death. This also explains active (action) versus passive speech. A person who states on social media, "I hate black people because they talk funny" is significantly different from another person who states, "I would like to kill a bunch of niggers." The first comment would fall under hostility speech, and the second would fall under hate speech. The first is not assumed criminal, but the second is criminal.

In 2022, there were more than six hundred mass shootings in the United States. Mass shootings are defined as four or more people injured or killed at one shooting, usually using a variant of an automatic gun. There is a correlation between hate speech and social media.

It seems rational and logical that if we had laws for hate speech that produces violence, but no laws for hostility speech, we would have a safer, more civilized America. But the argument is not the hate speech; it is mental health. This is like the Second Amendment saying it's not the guns, but the mental health of the person using the AR-15. If we eliminated automatic and military-style guns, recognize mental health disorders like conduct disorder, and had laws against hate speech, we would live in a civilized America. We have law enforcement in our communities to keep us safe—then why not cyber-police to keep us safe? One cannot argue that this proposition is autocratic since we allow for freedom of speech and enforcement just as we do with community law enforcement.

HATE CRIMES

Bias-motivated crime—or what we commonly refer to as hate crime—is a prejudice-motivated crime that occurs when a perpetrator targets a victim because of their membership (or perceived membership) of a certain social, sexual/gender, or racial group. The most common are race (Black, Asian), religion (Muslim, Jewish), and sexual or gender identity (LGBTQ).

Hate crimes correspond to standard crimes such as homicide, but the motivation is a result of hatred. These crimes associated with hatred include destruction of property (fire or bombs), bodily harm, homicide, hate mail, and hate graffiti. There is variability from country to country. A hate crime law is intended to deter bias-motivated violence. Hate crime laws are separate and more enforceable than hate speech laws in some countries.

What causes a person to cross the line from hatred to committing a hate crime? A study addressing the motivation of haters to commit a hate crime described four motives: thrill-seekers, defensive, retaliatory, and mission offenders.

THRILL-SEEKERS

Of the four motives, thrill-seeking accounted for 66 percent for all motives. The hate was already present, but the adrenaline rush and drama of carrying out the crime was highly motivating for some people. They also find vulnerability of the target, which sends a message to all his haters that this is justified. They usually pick places like churches, synagogues, gay bars and so forth to make their debut because the vulnerability is highest—and there are more targets.

DEFENSIVE

The perpetrators believe they are protecting their families and communities from the perceived danger from Black people, gay persons, Jews, and so forth. Events such as "Gay Pride" may trigger a crime by one or more individuals. Their delusional thinking makes them believe the rest of the community supports their actions.

RETALIATORY

The hate crime is committed when the perpetrator has the perceived feeling the person or group they hate has attacked them in some way. This can also be in retaliation for a previous hate crime or terrorism. The avengers target members of a group they believe committed the original crime—even if the victims had nothing to do with it. This kind of hate crimes are common after terrorist attacks.

MISSION OFFENDERS

This motive is due to ideological reasons. They consider themselves to be crusaders, often for a religious or racial cause. They frequently write complex explanations of their views and target sites on social media. This is often done to show persons in the hate group his intentions. This shows there is no other way than the crime to accomplish their goals. Their published material justifies the violence. This kind of hate crime often overlaps with terrorism, and it is considered by the FBI to be both the rarest and deadliest form of hate crime.

Hate crime laws generally fall into specific bias-motivated crimes or civil action toward hate crimes. In some countries, the laws cover war, genocide, and crimes against humanity.

Europe's hate crime laws range from no laws in Georgia to very specific laws in Ukraine. Many have penalties, but very few provide the amount of time for imprisonment.

In Belgium, the Centre for Equal Opportunities and the Fight against Racism established a penalty enhancement for crimes involving discrimination on the basis of gender, supposed race, color, descent, national or ethnic origin, sexual orientation, civil status, birth, fortune, age, religious or philosophical beliefs, current or future state of health, and handicap or physical features.

The Croatian Penal Code explicitly defines hate crime in article 89 as "any crime committed out of hatred for someone's race, skin color, sex, sexual orientation, language, religion, political or other belief, national or social background, asset, birth, education, social condition, age, health condition or other attribute."

In France, they have a penalty-enhancement hate crime laws for crimes motivated by bias against the victim's actual or perceived ethnicity, nation, race, religion, or sexual orientation. Imprisonment is starting at thirty years for murder, and violent attacks leading to permanent disability call for imprisonment for fifteen years.

Ukraine's specific hate crime laws include Article 161:

> Violations of equality of citizens depending on their race, ethnicity, religious beliefs, disability and other grounds: Intentional acts aimed at incitement to ethnic, racial or religious hatred and violence, to demean the ethnic honor and dignity, or to repulse citizens' feelings due to their religious beliefs, as well as direct or indirect restriction of rights or the establishment of direct or indirect privileges of citizens on the grounds of race, color, political, religious or other beliefs, sex, disability, ethnic or social origin, property status, place of residence, language or other grounds.

The maximum criminal sentence is up to eight years in prison.

Hate crime laws have a long history in the United States. The first hate crime laws were passed after the American Civil war, beginning with the Civil Rights Act of 1871. This was due to the racial violence against the post-war period, which also created the white supremacist group, the Ku Klux Klan. The Civil Rights Act was expanded in 1968, which meant that prosecution would come from the U.S. attorney general.

The first state hate-crime statute was passed in California in 1978. It included religion, color, and national origin. Other states followed with their own laws. Washington included ancestry in a statute that was passed in 1981. Alaska included creed and sex in 1982 and later added disability, sexual orientation, and ethnicity.

The Anti-Defamation League (ADL) became involved in hate crime laws. ADL drafted model hate crimes legislation in the 1980s that served as a template for the legislation that a majority of states have adopted. By 2020, forty-six states and the District of Columbia had statutes criminalizing various types of hate crimes, and 50–66 percent of these states keep statistical records on hate crimes.

The state of Georgia was one that did not incorporate hate crimes. In May 2020, the killing of African-American jogger Ahmaud Arbery reinvigorated efforts to adopt a hate crimes law in Georgia. The few other states without hate crime laws also incorporated hate crime laws into their criminal laws.

The statistics collected by each state on hate crimes are submitted to the FBI. The FBI reported that hate crimes for 2006 increased nearly 8 percent nationwide, with a total of 7,722 incidents and 9,080 offenses reported by participating law enforcement agencies. Of the 5,449 crimes against persons, 46 percent were classified as intimidation, and 32 percent were simple assaults. Acts of vandalism or destruction comprised 81 percent of the 3,593 crimes against property.

A report in 2009 revealed that 33 percent of hate crime offenders were under the age of eighteen, and 29 percent were between the ages of eighteen and twenty-four.

The 2011 hate crime statistics show 46.9 percent were motivated by race, and 20.8 percent were motivated by sexual orientationhttps://en.wikipedia.org/wiki/Hate_crime.

In 2015, the Hate Crimes Statistics report identified 5,818 single-bias incidents involving 6,837 offenses, 7,121 victims, and 5,475 known offenders.

In 2017, the FBI released new data showing a 17 percent increase in hate crimes between 2016 and 2017.

In 2018, the Hate Crime Statistics report showed 59.5 percent were motivated by race bias.

According to a 2021 study, in the years between 1992 and 2014, white people were the offenders in 74.5 percent of anti-Asian hate crimes, 99 percent of anti-Black hate crimes, and 81.1 percent of anti-Hispanic hate crimes.

Prosecutions have also been on the rise over the past decade. Most of them have been against members of the Ku Klux Klan and—starting in 2021—indictments against members of the Oath Keepers and Proud Boys for heir insurrection of Capitol on January 6, 2020.

After September 11, 2001, terrorist attacks, the United States experienced a spike in overall hate crimes against Muslim individuals. In the year before, only twenty-eight hate crimes against Muslims had been recorded; in 2001, the number jumped to 481. While the number decreased in the following years, since Donald Trump's presidency, the number of Muslim hate crimes has been higher than before 2001.

Statistics show that 74 percent of hate crimes in America are committed by white people. Much of the hate crimes were directed against race, but there was a rise crime against those who had different sexual orientations.

The Hate Crime Prevention Act, signed into law in 2009, included sexual orientation, gender identity and expression, disability status, and military personnel and their family members.

Also, during Donald Trump's time in office, hate crimes against transgender individuals rose. There are several reasons why there is limited news reporting on the deaths of the victims in the trans community. Studies indicate the trans community experiences hate crime due to lack of family acceptance, hostile political climate, and cultural marginalization. These factors can have various effects on a trans individual, including homelessness, employment discrimination, and health care risks.

As result of Donald Trump's rhetoric, in June 2020, the deaths of several African Americans at the hands of police officers—in particular, George Floyd—triggered protests around the world as part of the Black Lives Matter movement.

DR. DANIEL BRUBAKER

THE PSYCHOLOGICAL EFFECTS OF HATE CRIMES AND HATE SPEECH

Hate crimes and hate speech have significant and a wide spectrum of psychological consequences on the victim and others around them. These disorders include substance abuse, somatization, anxiety, depression, acute post-traumatic stress disorder, chronic post-traumatic stress disorder, complex traumatic stress disorder, and suicide. In every situation, there is fear for the victim and for those around them.

The trauma of hate-based violence differs from other types of traumas. The assaults or deprivation of resources carried out through hate-based violence are intended to send a message to the survivors and to their actual or perceived groups.

Studies have found that gay and lesbian victims of violent hate crimes are psychologically vulnerable and experience higher levels of psychological distress, including anxiety and depression. Hypervigilance and post-traumatic stress disorder are also common.

Survivors of hate crimes often feel powerlessness, isolation, guilt, shame, anger, and loss of faith in law enforcement.

The impact of prejudice and discrimination may extend beyond the trauma associated with criminal victimization and frequently challenge the survivor's self-esteem. This is especially true of LGBTQ and gender identification victims. This is heightened if the victim is a different race or culture. This can be even more traumatic for younger people without parental or family support. For parents who support their children's gender identification, there is constant anxiety relating to the safety of their children and a perceived inability to protect them. They feel powerlessness, anger, shame, and frustration due to the effects of prejudice and discrimination.

The impact on the individual is dependent upon the severity of the crime and the number of encounters the person experiences. The psychological impact also affects members of the targeted group, causing insecurity, vulnerability, and loss of self-esteem.

Divisions and factionalism arising in response to hate crimes are particularly damaging to cultural, ethnic, and religious communities, such as Muslims and Jewish people. Terrorism and mass killings affect entire communities. Hypervigilance and complex traumatic stress disorders occur.

Elementary and high school mass shootings are hate crimes. These crimes were conducted by teenage boys who had conduct disorders. There is anger, aggression, and hatred in conduct disorders, which allow a teenage boy with an AR-15 military rifle to kill a large number of children and teachers.

The first major mass school shooting was in Littleton, Colorado. It was the largest and deadliest mass school shooting in US history at that time, which occurred on April 20, 1999 at Columbine High School.

The shootings were carried out by Eric Harris, age eighteen, and Dylan Klebold, age seventeen. On April 20, 1999, they entered Columbine High School with semiautomatic rifles, pistols, and several explosives. In less than twenty minutes, they killed twelve fellow students and a teacher and wounded twenty-one others. The violence came to an end when Harris and Klebold took their own lives, making it a total of fifteen deaths.

The Sandy Hook Elementary shooting took place in Newtown, Connecticut, on December 14, 2012. There were twenty-seven victims: twenty-one first-graders and six adult teachers. Between 2012 to present time, there were more than one thousand mass school shootings.

The next major school shooting was in Parkland, Florida, at Marjory Stoneman Douglas High School on February 14, 2018, killing seventeen students and teachers with attempts to kill seventeen more. Four years later, on November 2, 2022, a jury found Nicholas Cruz guilty of the crime, but instead of giving him the death penalty, they gave him life in prison.

On May 24, 2022, the largest school shooting occurred in Uvalde, Texas. Nineteen children and two teachers were killed with a military-style rifle. A teenage male killed his grandmother and then went to Robb Elementary School and killed twenty-one victims. Many police officers stood outside the school for seventy minutes before entering the school and killing the shooter. There were issues with the school board and mayor of Uvalde as well. The governor of Texas, Greg Abbott, was also negligent in his duties.

The grieving process in families of mass murders of children is much different from the grieving process reported in chapter 2. The grieving process of a child dying from cancer is different from a child dying from a mass school shooting. The grieving process lasts much longer in families where mass shootings occurred. The mental state and mental status over time of the deceased victim's families and survivals of these heinous military-style murders are multifactorial. There is no doubt that the survivors have post-traumatic stress disorders and complex traumatic stress disorders. The family members have anxiety and depression that lasts for years. There are a few who committed suicide. Some grow closer to their faith.

The most prominent emotion is anger. We see more assertive anger with families from the Parkland and Uvalde school shootings. When mass killer in Parkland, Nicholas Cruz, was sentenced, there was a clear display of anger by the victims' families in the courtroom when he was only sentenced to life in prison, rather than the death penalty.

The families of the murdered children in Uvalde had immediate anger toward all of law enforcement for not responding immediately and stopping the shooter from murdering so many children. That anger has continued for years because there has not been any accountability for the negligence of law enforcement, the government, or the governor.

Passive anger is also present in pockets of families and students displayed by protesting and petitioning lawmakers and the United States government to enact gun laws. Connecticut Senator Chris Murphy and President Obama tried to pass laws after the Sandy Hook shootings in Newtown Connecticut National Rifle Association blocked their efforts in Congress.

After the Parkland shooting, the students from the high school became active protestors against lawmakers to pass stricter gun laws.

Within six weeks of the shooting, on March 24, 2018, the March for Our Lives protest took place. It is considered the most famous youth movement in recent history—with approximately two million attendees in more than eight hundred cities around the world.

Emma "X" González and David Hogg organized the march. They also used social media and established a national debate about school safety and gun control by directly confronting legislators and speaking truth to power in spite of the negative backlash they faced. Since Parkland, there have been more than fifty-gun control laws in the United States state legislatures.

After the Uvalde shooting, the US Senate passed the Safer Communities Act, which required background checks, mental health evaluations for teenagers, and other mental health services in the communities. It provides support for school safety and many more protections against gun violence. In some states, the most obvious one was to change the age of gun sales from eighteen to twenty-one. Nevertheless, there is more work to be done to prevent more mass murders.

SUMMARY

There is some form of grief resulting from the actions of hate. Let us consider bullying in schools and politics. A strong, aggressive child might bully a weaker child. The bully finds pleasure in overpowering his victim and causing physical or verbal pain. This causes a grieving process in the victim in the form of crying, denial, depression, and anger. Over time, the anger turns into hate, and the victim may seek revenge and retaliate when he is older and stronger. The hate is evident in both the one who inflicts pain and the one who suffers.

Therefore, hatred has very bad consequences for both parties. This emotion can be directed to individuals, groups, or objects that cause discomfort or hurt us. Hate is often associated with feelings of anger, disgust, and a deep disappointment toward those who are hostile to us.

Hate can be the cause of grief in many situations, which is the purpose of this chapter. It can be a cycle of hate causing grief and the response can sometimes cause hate. This also represents issues regarding the forgiveness process as a result of many complex and complicated factors.

CHAPTER 8
CONCLUSION OF GRIEF AND FORGIVENESS

We only summarize grief and forgiveness because they are associated with each other. This book is intended to help people in their grieving process. Pain, suffering, and grieving are inevitable in every human being. Grieving occurs with a loss, such as getting fired from a job, divorce, death of a pet or loved one.

Dr. Kubler-Ross wrote the book on Death and Dying. She created five stages of grief; denial, anger, betrayal, depression, and acceptance. With grieving, these stages are never in order. We agree with these stages, but added shock as the first stage and moving on as the last stage. We further describe each of these stages. Each person processes grief differently. There is no one method to come to terms with grief.

SHOCK

Shock is defined as a sudden upsetting or traumatic experience. A sudden loss causes shock. We think shock is the first stage of grief from a sudden loss. As a result of a sudden loss and shock, one may feel numb, denial, or anger.

Shock frequently incorporates crying. Crying is a gift given to us by God, and no other mammal has the ability to shed tears. Animals can make sounds and whimper. We hear this when a dog is in pain or when they lose another dog they are attached to.

Emotional crying is biologically complex due to the involvement of hormones and neurochemicals. Crying releases several chemicals and hormones that can affect the parasympathetic nervous system, which decreases heart rate and breathing, relaxes the body, causes a soothing effect, and calms emotions. With support from others, the crying person relaxes as an attachment behavior. Crying may help lift a person's spirits and make them feel better. The calming, mood-enhancing, and pain-relieving effects of crying may help a person fall asleep more easily. Oxytocin and endorphins can help improve mood. This is why they are often known as "feel good" chemicals.

We can see that the biochemistry and physiology of crying causes a calming effect, making us feel better. Therefore, no one should interfere with a person who is crying. by saying, "please don't cry!" One should cry for as long as they want and as frequently, as it will help them feel better. People want the person crying to stop because it makes them feel bad, but compassion should allow the person to cry.

DENIAL

Denial is another stage in grieving. A person might deny the existence, truth, or validity of something despite proof or strong evidence that it is real, true, and valid. *The Oxford Dictionary* defines it as the action of declaring something to be untrue. A person who is in denial often is struggling to accept something that seems overwhelming or stressful. However, in the short term, this defense mechanism can have a useful purpose. It can allow one to have time to adjust to a sudden change in one's reality.

In psychology, denial is a type of defense mechanism that involves ignoring the reality of a situation to avoid anxiety. Defense mechanisms are strategies that people use to cope with distressing feelings. In the case of denial, it can involve not acknowledging reality or denying the consequences of that reality.

In denial, one avoids facing stress, conflict, threats, or, and anxieties.

The two main situations in which denial occurs in grief are after the unexpected death of a loved one or after being diagnosed with a chronic or terminal disease. With the death of a loved one, a person might refuse to accept the reality of the death and deny that anything has happened. In the second situation, a person might refuse to believe that the problem is as serious as it really is. They might think, *I'll get over it. it can't be that bad.* Unfortunately, denial can potentially interfere with treatment.

The grieving person in denial may not talk about the situation. They feel hopeless and helpless, and they refuse to accept help. The denial defense mechanism can be an attempt to avoid uncomfortable realities (such as grief), anxiety, truths, distressing or painful situations, unpleasant feelings, or traumatic events.

Denial should not necessarily be considered bad. In the process of dealing with something shocking or distressing, denial can give one a little time and space to gradually, often unconsciously, come to grips with the change. In grieving a loved one's death, it provides time to accept the reality of the death.

In a personal health issue, one might be in denial because one doesn't want to face the possibility of being seriously ill. Rather than needlessly worrying, being in denial can give one a little time to come to terms and remain calm while seeking care. Getting treatment while being in denial can prevent worrying.

ANGER

Why is there anger in the grieving process? Anger is defined as an intense emotional state involving a strong uncomfortable and noncooperative response to a perceived provocation, hurt, or threat. It may also be called wrath, like the wrath of God, or rage. Anger is especially incorporated into normative and ideological hatred.

Anger can be expressed as a mild to severe emotion. At all levels, anger can be expressed toward oneself or another.

The physiology of moderate to severe anger is similar to that of fear. Adrenaline (epinephrine) and norepinephrine are released to cause increased heart rate, blood pressure, and breathing. It is similar to the fight-or-flight response of fear

Anger, when viewed as a protective response or instinct to a perceived threat, is considered positive. The negative expression of this state is known as aggression. Acting on this misplaced state is rage due to potential errors in perception and judgment.

Anger causes a reduction in cognitive ability. Perception is inaccurate, and external stimuli have indiscriminate perception. Real danger seems less risky, and there is more risk in making decisions. In terms of intergroup relationships, anger makes people think about outsiders in more negative and prejudiced terms.

Goodness, empathy, and forgiveness can develop from anger. Nothing good can come from hate because hate takes possession of the hater. If you hate someone or something, you have placed what you hate beyond compassion and understanding. The hated person becomes an object.

Anger in grief can be directed toward the situation, the diseased person, the perpetrator, the self, or God. Anger may be in the form of situational fear of being alone when a loved one dies. When a loved one dies, anger may occur at the diseased mother who can no longer experience the son's wedding, graduation, childbirth, and so forth.

Gun violence has caused anger toward the shooters. This can be from parents who lost their child in a school shooting, which is directed toward the shooter, police, governor, or legislators. A prime example is the school shooting in Nashville, Tennessee. The three Democrats in the legislature protested with students and families in the community, which led to their expulsion from the statehouse. This was a huge community protest. Another example is the Black Lives Matter protest over George Floyd's death by police officers.

Getting sick, developing a chronic disease, or having a terminal illness can lead to anger in the form of fear or sadness. The duration of this anger may be days or months. Crying can also occur in this stage.

Grief from trauma can lead to anger with God. This may also occur with terminal illness. We see God as having control of our lives, and when we lose control, we blame God. This comes in the form of anger. Another way of evaluating this is that one regains power over sadness and fear.

One should feel the anger, but at some point, they must address this stage. Suppressing anger can only lead to more problems, such as isolation, rage, and hate. Suppressing anger can lead to bitterness, resentment, hostility, and loss of friends and family because they don't want to be with you.

BARGAINING

The Oxford Dictionary defines bargaining as negotiating the terms and conditions of a transaction or parting with something after negotiating—but getting little or nothing in return. The key word in bargaining is negotiation.

According to the American Psychological Association, in the bargaining stage one may try to negotiate with oneself or with a higher power to try to undo the loss. Some people attempt to postpone sadness by imagining what-if scenarios. They also feel guilt or responsibility due to the loss, which leads to bargaining for ways to prevent more emotional pain or future losses.

In a divorce, one person might say, "If only I had spent more time with her, she would have stayed." After being fired from a job, they might say, "I should have been on time for work" or "If only I worked more weekends!" With a death of a loved one, they might say, "If only I had spent more time with her!"

This is also the stage where we bargain with God for whatever reason. I did this as a child when I had a bad case of the measles. I asked God to keep me from dying by joining the church and being baptized in a creek on a cold spring day.

Bargaining is probably the shortest stage of grieving. It may be episodic, but it does not last very long. It is more passive than active.

DEPRESSION

Depression is usually the longest and most difficult stage of grief. In this long and difficult stage of the grieving process, many people feel their deepest sadness.

As a result of a significant loss, a person often enters a state of depression once the reality of the loss has been realized. The person becomes overwhelmed with sadness. They feel like they don't deserve the loss. Life feels like it is unfair. When the going gets tough, they want to give up. It is difficult to realize that life has significantly changed.

Depression is often associated with anger. Repressed anger can show up in the form of depression. If grief is the process of healing, then depression is the evidence of one's progress on this journey.

The symptoms of depression in grief may be mild. One may experience sadness and function normally at the same time. However, one may not want to be around many people or have difficulty getting up in the morning. The difference between clinical depression and depression in grief is that one is totally isolated in clinical depression.

The symptoms of depression can be complex and vary widely between people. With depression, one may feel sad, helpless, or hopeless and lose interest in things they used to enjoy.

The psychological symptoms of depression include guilt, indecision, loss of motivation, few interests, little enjoyment, no appetite, poor sleep and hygiene, and unexplained aches and pains.

ACCEPTANCE

Acceptance in grief is a very gradual acceptance of the new way of life and a feeling of possibility in the future.

Acceptance is considered the last of the five stages of grief, but we consider the last stage as moving on with life. All the stages of grieving may return at intervals. Acceptance does not necessarily mean the whole grieving process no longer exists.

Acceptance in grief means embracing the present—considered bad—in order to shape the future. It does not mean that we no longer can think about the horrific or terrible incident or the death of a loved one. Out of sight does not have to mean out of mind since the brain has a strong memory.

An excellent professional reference for persons who are grieving is called Choosing Therapy. This group has an extensive list of mental health professionals.

ADDITIONAL RESOURCES

Online Therapy and BetterHelp
Choosing Therapy
Mental Health America
National Alliance on Mental Health
MentalHealth.gov
The Compassionate Friends
The Dougy Center for Grieving Children and Families

Grieving.com
Acceptance Stage of Grief

MOVING ON

In the last stage of the seven stages of grief, moving on is considered reconstruction. We see reconstruction occurring with acceptance. Moving on means moving out of the pain stage and into functional living.

Merriam-Webster defines moving on in life to continue living one's life in the usual way after all the problems they've had recently. When one moves on in life, it is usually in the form of perseverance when the right choice is made. Perseverance is the persistence in doing something despite difficulty.

Acceptance and moving on are intertwined with perseverance. One can be in denial and move on with life, which could serve as a defense mechanism. I remember during my stage 4 colon cancer, I moved on with working and mountain biking as if nothing else was happening in my life. I also read Dr. Chopra's book on healing.

Does that mean moving on is the same as acceptance? No! One can move on and persevere without accepting the painful situation. Functioning without acceptance is difficult and may have associated mild depression. Certainly in severe depression, one is not moving on.

The human brain is amazing at moving on. We see people in the worst disaster, whether it is a flood, a tornado, an earthquake, persevere and rebuild whatever was destroyed. In these situations, one doesn't rebuild everything alone; they have a lot of help. The same should also be true with a loss of a loved one.

Along with perseverance should come commitment. Commitment is the precursor to perseverance. After a disaster, the first thoughts are commitment. This is the statement of rebuilding whatever has been destroyed. This can also be the start of moving on.

Moving on in grief can be confusing for others. Usually, "move on" is said by other people around the grieving person. It generally means to stop hurting, stop talking about it, stop crying, stop remembering, stop grieving, and so forth. Others want the hurting person to stop grieving because they don't want to feel the pain. It is not a happy experience for either person. The grieving person frequently becomes isolated by others, yet part of the healing process is to be with and talk to others. It's a catch-22. It becomes a choice for the grieving person to choose empathetic persons to talk to about one's grief.

When the going gets tough, the tough get going! Moving on is not about being weak or strong. Those who are perceived as weak can "mount up with wings of eagles!" Those who are perceived as strong may struggle with moving on.

Coping with grief is not easy. It is better said than done. Life goes on, and the alternative is not an option. Under acceptance, one can be educated with all the options of coping.

Coping means dealing with something difficult. It does not mean elimination of grief with one of the stages. In medicine, there are some diseases that are cured, but there are many more that aren't. In those that are not cured, as physicians, we try to improve the quality of life—along with longevity. Grief is similar in which it may not be cured, but with help, quality of life can be significantly improved.

Another consideration that is not discussed much is coping for the elderly. With old age, one is reaching closer to death. I have experience in elderly patients' significant anxiety with aging. The ability to cope with life becomes more difficult. It makes sense that as one reaches their own mortality, rumination with the face of death becomes real. This is true even in those who are in good health.

FORGIVENESS

Forgiveness can be included in the grieving process. If the loved one who died was sometimes not very nice to his or her spouse, forgiveness toward the diseased person can occur. If a person killed your child, one could forgive the shooter. However, a really deep, sincere apology would need to take place. This one is difficult, but it is possible. There are many scenarios for this situation. The benefit of these scenarios is that one can now release anger and hostility. The goal of forgiveness as defined is to stop feeling angry or resentful toward someone for an offense, flaw, or mistake. Forgiveness does not necessarily eliminate grieving, but it helps reduce some of the symptoms of grieving.

Exoneration forgiveness is complete forgiveness where hard feelings, grudges, dislike, fear, anger, hostility, and resentment are all totally gone. This releases any anger or resentment. This can be as simple as someone causing hard feelings to the other, but they apologize—and then there is forgiveness. It can also be more complex. If someone causes another to lose their job, the person may feel extremely bad, apologize, and ask for forgiveness. In certain situations, the person who hurt you is truly sorry, takes full responsibility (without excuses) for what they did, asks forgiveness, and gives you confidence that they will not knowingly repeat their bad action in the future.

Forbearance forgiveness is when an offender either makes a partial apology or lessens their apology by suggesting that the person who is hurt is also partially to blame for their wrongdoing. This appears and feels like the wrongdoer's forgiveness is not authentic. This is where someone might say, "I apologize for what I did, but you should not have done what you did too." Still, the wronged should forgive but not forget. In the exoneration type, there is legitimacy, authenticity, and respect. It is a warm feeling that does not require vigilance like forbearance requires. However, in some cases, after a sufficient period of good behavior, forbearance can rise to exoneration and full forgiveness.

Threatening forgiveness is conditional or absent. The wronged may say, "I'll forgive you if you stop hurting me." The forgiveness from the wrongdoer or wronged is preceded by "if." The wrongdoer does not even acknowledge that they have done anything wrong or gives an obviously insincere apology, making no reparations whatsoever. The wrongdoer will absolutely provide the wronged with an apology or ask for forgiveness. These wrongdoers usually have a mental health disorder, such as narcissism.

Release type forgiveness does not exonerate the wrongdoer or require forbearance. There is no further need for a relationship. However, it does require the wronged to release the hurt. The preoccupation, rumination, and anger will require mental release from all of these negative thoughts, so that mental health is restored. One is now free of the heavy burden of hurt, pain betrayal, and anger. By definition, this is really the essence of forgiveness: releasing the anger. We may experience release when someone, for example, has murdered a spouse or killed your child with fentanyl. However, dwelling on the hurt only allows for the wrongdoer to be attached to the mind, which is not healthy. First, one must be aware that maintaining the hurt is harmful. Knowing that, one can move forward with counselling, psychotherapy, or talking with someone who can be trusted.

EXAMPLES OF FORGIVENESS FROM FAMOUS PEOPLE

One of the famous persons to provide public forgiveness was Bill Clinton's forgiveness to Americans over his affair with Monica Lewinsky.

President Clinton had an affair with Lewinsky for about eighteen months. The scandal reached the media when he was involved in a lawsuit regarding the sexual scandal with Paula Jones.

The US House of Representatives, run by Republicans, investigated the Lewinsky scandal in 1998. He ended a television speech in January 1998 with the later infamous statement: "I did not have sexual relations with that woman, Ms. Lewinsky." However, a detailed investigation proved he did have sexual relations with Ms. Lewinsky. This led to impeachment proceedings as a result of lying under oath. He was subsequently acquitted on all impeachment charges of perjury and obstruction.

In a speech from the White House Oval Office on August 17, 1998, Bill Clinton offered an apology to the American people: "Now, this matter is between me, the two people I love most—my wife and our daughter—and our God. I must put it right, and I am prepared to do whatever it takes to do so. Nothing is more important to me personally. But it is private, and I intend to reclaim my family life for my family. It's nobody's business but ours."

In a news conference with Russian President Yeltsin in Moscow on September 2, 1998, President Clinton said, "I have acknowledged that I made a mistake, said that I regretted it, asked to be forgiven, spent a lot of very valuable time with my family in the last couple of weeks and said I was going back to work. I believe that's what the American people want me to do, and based on my conversations with leaders around the world, I think that's what they want me to do, and that is what I intend to do. And I'm going to do my best to continue to go through this personal process in an appropriate way, but to do my job, to do the job I was hired to do. And I think it very much needs to be done right now. I think the question of the tone of the speech and people's reaction to it is really a function of—I can't comment on that. I read it the other day again, and I thought it was clear that I was expressing my profound regret to all who were hurt and to all who were involved, and my desire not to see any more people hurt by this process and caught up in it."

The American people did not approve of his apologies, resulting in his poll ratings dropping. He gave another apology publicly that used religion. In essence, he asked God to forgive him for his wrongdoing.

The first two public apologies were more or less threatening types of forgiveness. Please forgive me, but this is nobody's business, because it's a private matter. It is also a manipulative political forgiveness. The one asking God's forgiveness, which the Americans really accepted was a submissive forgiveness. Nevertheless, both were misplaced. The exoneration forgiveness would have been to publicly offer forgiveness to Ms. Lewinsky for how the media bullied her. Also, a public apology, under the circumstances, to his wife would have been better than to the American people. In the author's opinion, he did not need to apologize to the American people because he did no harm to them.

A great forgiveness was made by Nelson Mandela. Nelson Mandela was born in South Africa on July 18, 1918, and died on

GRIEF, FORGIVENESS, ACCEPTANCE, AND REJECTION

December 5, 2013. He fought for racial and social justice. He studied law and worked as a lawyer in Johannesburg where he became an African nationalist politics and an activist against colonialism. He joined the African National Congress (ANC) in 1943. He had significant defiance against the National Party's white-only government-established apartheid, a system of racial segregation of privileged whites from Black Africans.

Nelson Mandela was repeatedly arrested for seditious activities and was unsuccessfully prosecuted in the 1956 Treason Trial. Mandela continued his path to overthrow the National Party government, which led to his arrest and imprisonment in 1962. He was sentenced to life imprisonment for conspiring to overthrow the state.

Mandela served twenty-seven years in prison, in solitary confinement and terrible conditions, and he also acquired tuberculosis. During his imprisonment, there was pressure to release him over concerns about a racial civil war. President F.W. de Kleck released him in 1990. Mandela and de Kleck led efforts to negotiate an end to apartheid.

Mandela stayed in prison for twenty-seven years. But rather than being resentful when he came out, he forgave everyone. "Revenge is not the solution. Forgiveness is the only way forward."

A fully democratic multiracial election was held in 1994. Mandela served as the first Black president of South Africa from 1994 to 1999. President Mandela emphasized reconciliation between the country's racial groups and created the Truth and Reconciliation Commission to oversee human rights abuses.

Mandela later emphasized personal forgiveness and reconciliation. He announced, "Courageous people do not fear forgiving, for the sake of peace." Nelson Mandela also said, "Forgiveness liberates the soul, it removes fear. That's why it's such a powerful weapon."

Mandela's forgiveness fits into the exoneration type of forgiveness.

There are all kinds of forgiveness, such as dismissive, graceful, political, manipulative, religious, and so forth. The five types we outlined are submissive, exoneration, forbearance, threatening, and release.

In this chapter, we combined grief and forgiveness to add more detail. There is an overlap between the two concerning the emotions involved. Both require the same coping skills. Both require professional help when there is interference with the person's ability to function.

There is so much hate, pain, and suffering in our lives. The intent of this book has been to help us all break through these negative emotions and find functionality and ultimately reach happiness.

Printed in the USA
CPSIA information can be obtained
at www.ICGtesting.com
LVHW090313280824
789407LV00005B/165/J